MIRACLE MOMENTS
IN
NEW YORK METS
HISTORY

Miracle Moments in NEW YORK METS History

The Turning Points, the Memorable Games, the Incredible Records

BY BRETT TOPEL

SPORTS
PUBLISHING

Sports Publishing books may be purchased in bulk at special discounts for sales promotion, corporate gifts, fund-raising, or educational purposes. Special editions can also be created to specifications. For details, contact the Special Sales Department, Sports Publishing, 307 West 36th Street, 11th Floor, New York, NY 10018 or sportspubbooks@skyhorsepublishing.com.

Sports Publishing® is a registered trademark of Skyhorse Publishing, Inc.®, a Delaware corporation.

Visit our website at www.sportspubbooks.com.

10 9 8 7 6 5 4 3 2 1

Library of Congress Cataloging-in-Publication Data is available on file.

All interior photos by AP Images, unless otherwise noted.

Cover design by Kai Texel
Cover photo credit: Getty Images

ISBN: 978-1-68358-422-3
Ebook ISBN: 978-1-68358-206-9

Printed in China

This book is dedicated to the memory of my grandparents,
who continue to inspire me every day.

By DelaywavesⅠ courtesy of Wikimedia Commons

Contents

PREFACE

In June 2018, this book was originally released highlighting 31 special moments that were, no doubt, all too familiar to Mets fans. If you are like me, you will enjoy taking a step back in time to read about these exciting moments, many of which include new perspectives and firsthand accounts.

It was time to freshen the book up, however, so this updated edition has brand-new chapters on Jacob deGrom's back-to-back Cy Young seasons in 2018 and 2019 and Pete Alonso's magical rookie campaign in 2019, as well as this preface. *Miracle Moments in New York Mets History* now spans nearly 60 years of Mets history and has something for everyone who pulls for the blue and orange.

One of the things about rooting for a team is the relationship that develops between the fans and the radio and television announcers. The way that the announcers describe the action often becomes what we remember first about many of these miracle moments. From 1962 through 1978 only three men—Ralph Kiner, Bob Murphy, and Lindsey Nelson—called every Mets game, alternating between television and radio. In recent years, the close bond between announcers and fans has continued with Howie Rose and Wayne Randazzo on radio and Gary Cohen, Keith Hernandez, and Ron Darling on television. The relationship is more than just that of announcer and fan, however. Considering how much time Mets fans spend with these voices during the baseball seasons—which add up over the years—the relationship becomes something much more familial. How the game is called can truly influence how we remember particular plays, specific games, and individual moments. That is especially true when it comes to Rose and Cohen, who are lifelong Mets fans and can relate full well to their fellow fans in good times and bad.

Never before was that close relationship more evident than in the days that followed the death of Mets legend Tom Seaver—without a doubt the most tragic

Mets moment since this book was originally published. When Seaver died in September 2020, the entire Mets community was stunned. One year earlier, Seaver's family announced that because the Hall of Famer was suffering from dementia he would no longer appear in public. However, when Seaver passed away at the age of 75, it was almost too much to take. Tributes poured in from throughout baseball—and beyond—as the man known as "The Franchise" truly transcended baseball.

The first time the Mets took the field after Seaver's death, every member of the Mets had a dirt smudge on their right knee—a tribute to how Tom often had that same smudge on his pants thanks to his drop-and-drive style of pitching. The Mets were trailing the New York Yankees in the bottom of the ninth inning before J. D. Davis homered off closer Aroldis Chapman to tie the game. Then, in the bottom of the 10th, Pete Alonso stepped to the plate with Dom Smith, the automatic runner, on second base. The fact that Alonso ripped a ball into the left-field stands at Citi Field for the walk-off win was dramatic and thrilling, however, it was what happened in the Mets radio booth that was most touching. While Wayne Randazzo made the home run call on WCBS, his broadcast partner, Howie Rose, lifted his arms in jubilation, as if he was back in 1969 watching his Mets win a big game. Rose pumped both arms toward the skies in celebration, put his hands on his head, took his glasses off, and then he broke down, as the moment overtook him. He rubbed his eyes, was able to get one line out about Seaver authoring a great ending to the game, and motioned for Randazzo to continue talking. The death of Tom Seaver—his boyhood hero and former broadcasting colleague—was finally real.

"This was one of the most emotional days and games in 'Franchise' history and we'll remember it forever," Rose tweeted after the game, "but it would have meant so much more if you [the fans] were at the ballpark with us. [The fans] are so vitally important to the in-game experience and it was never more evident than today. 41"

While most are not as personal as the game following Seaver's death, emotional radio and television calls have been a part of Mets moments forever. Mets fans can relate to phrases such as *Little roller up along first*, *This one's got a chance*, and *He made the catch!* When the Mets hit a big home run, if you're watching on television, you expect to hear *Outta here! Outta here!* from Gary Cohen. And when the Mets win, if fans are listening on radio, they know that they can *Put it in the books!* thanks to Howie Rose. The truth is that the calls, in many cases, have become as much a part of these moments as the moments themselves. To that end, in many of the chapters you are about to read, the transcription of a radio or television call will be included to help bring the moment to life. Those calls, after all, are a part of the fabric of what it means to be a Mets fan. Hopefully, they will provide some extra enjoyment as you travel back throughout Mets history.

I want to thank several people who helped make this update possible, including SNY's Gary Apple and former Mets catcher Kevin Plawecki, who were both very generous with their time and sharing their memories.

PART ONE

REGULAR-SEASON MOMENTS

On the surface, it all seems so unimpressive. If you look at the Mets' all-time regular-season record you will see that entering the 2018 campaign the team had won 4,285 times and lost 4,647 times. To think the Mets will ever get back to .500 seems unlikely, even to the most ardent of fans. In order to make up the 362-game difference, the Mets would need to win around 95 or more games for about 13-straight seasons. But Mets fans know that they need to dig a little deeper. There is nothing "surface" about being a Mets fan. In fact, there's not a die-hard Mets fan around who would give back one of the times the Mets graduated from the regular season.

And at the end of the day, Mets fans tend to stick with their team.

Legendary New York *Daily News* columnist and cartoonist Bill Gallo once wrote:

Show me a dyed-in-the-wool Met fan, and I'll show you the most intense, most loyal, most baseball-savvy and tormented soul you're apt to find rooting in any stadium. This kind of Met fan has to be all these things because he has watched his beloved team reach the ultimate highs of glory and suffered through the terrible times when his club played like ragamuffins.

After suffering through a record of 394 wins and 737 losses in their first seven seasons, the Mets shocked the world by having a 1969 season that will never be forgotten. On their way to making an incredible regular-season comeback to catch the Chicago Cubs and win the National League East, Tom Seaver gave Mets fans a night to remember by flirting with perfection. That moment—one of three chapters that focus on Seaver—is just one of the 17 moments during the regular season that are featured in Part I of this book.

The following section covers the team's very first victory in 1962, as well as memorable moments from stars such as Willie Mays, Lee Mazzilli, Doc Gooden, Mike Piazza, Edgardo Alfonzo, Johan Santana, Bartolo Colón, and many more. Each of the Mets' six decades are represented with at least two moments, so Part I really includes something for every fan.

With that said, let's play ball!

1

Finally, a Win! (1962)

When you plunge into the history made by the New York Metropolitan Baseball Club, you cannot help but feel a familial connection to the makers of that history. Mets fans are among the most loyal fans there are, enduring plenty of ups and downs along the way—just like any family. There are good days, there are bad days, there are days you choose not to remember, and there are days that you will never forget.

On April 23, 2015, the New York Mets had a good day and defeated the Atlanta Braves by a score of 6–3. It was the team's 11th-straight victory and gave the first-place Mets a 13–3 mark on the young season. The winning pitcher for that game was a forty-one-year-old by the name of Bartolo Colón, who improved his record to 4 wins with no losses.

Ultimately that team, as all Mets fans well remember, went on to win the National League East and the National League pennant and fell just short of its ultimate goal, losing in the World Series to the Kansas City Royals. Those were memorable moments to be sure.

Six decades earlier, on April 23, 1962, the Mets were also looking to secure a victory—not to extend a winning streak but to end a rather dubious losing streak. They had already endured many days that they would choose not to remember. You see, on April 23 the Mets were getting set to play the 10th game of the season and—more specifically—the 10th game in team history. The thing is, they hadn't won yet.

The Mets were born out of the once vibrant National League baseball pres-ence in New York City long vacated by the Brooklyn Dodgers and New York Giants. When they created the baseball cap for the Mets, ownership decided to go with a mash-up of Dodgers blue and the orange interlocked NY that had once adorned the Giants' caps. The Mets were the new kids in town but not exactly new kids to baseball. Made up of well-past-their-prime veterans who all possessed turnstile-friendly names and some other guys who would never have a prime, the Mets were led by one of the most successful managers of all time.

Jay Hook earned the first-ever victory for the Mets.

While the 1962 roster would soon become known as Casey Stengel's lovable bunch of Mets, they were still professional baseball players. The lovable-losers label wouldn't come until much later on, and make no mistake, these men were not laughing at their 0–9 start.

"There was pressure with Casey because he didn't want to be embarrassed," said starting pitcher Jay Hook, who was drafted by the Mets from the Cincinnati Reds as the third pick in the premium phase of the 1961 expansion draft. "I am sure there was really more pressure on Casey than maybe on the players themselves. We had a bunch of guys who knew what they were doing, when you think of guys like Gil Hodges, Duke Snider, and Richie Ashburn. It was just a matter of time before we were going to win a game."

That time, it turned out, was on April 23, as unlikely as that may have seemed heading into Game 10 of the season. The Mets' opponent that night was the Pittsburgh Pirates, who had jumped out to a fast 10–0 record. The Pirates, led by guys like Roberto Clemente, Bill Mazeroski, and Dick Groat, among others, did not appear to have any use for the Mets, whom they had beaten five times already in 1962.

For the Mets, however, enough was enough. Or, quite possibly, the Baseball Gods had had enough fun for one April.

"One of the great things about baseball is that it's a new game everyday," said Hook, who was tapped to start the Mets' 10th game of the season.

Hook had pitched a strong eight innings in his first outing of the season, only to get a no-decision when the Mets lost to the Houston Colt .45s to drop to 0–5.

This time things would be different for Hook and the Mets, however, who scratched out an early 2–0 lead in the top of the first thanks to two sacrifice flies.

"The Pirates had a really good team, and we got out ahead of them," Hook remembered. "That made it a little easier."

For a team that in its first couple of weeks found nothing come easy, the floodgates opened at Forbes Field that night for the Mets. Even Hook, who played many different positions growing up, got into the hitting spree. It was Hook's two-run single that extended the Mets' lead to 4–0 in the top of the second inning.

"Early in spring training, Rogers Hornsby was one of our coaches," said Hook. Hornsby, of course, had been inducted into the Hall of Fame 20 years earlier and had a lifetime batting average of .358. He knew a thing or two about hitting. More specifically, he was one of the greatest hitters to ever live. "After some of our practices, I would ask Rogers if he would come into the batting cage, and I spent a lot of time practicing hitting and bunting. I wasn't a bad hitter in high school or in college, but the reason I did that was I thought that if they don't have to take me out for a pinch-hitter because I was an automatic out, I would have the chance to go deeper into games. So I had practiced my hitting a lot. I went up expecting to get a hit, even though I didn't get too many. I didn't want to be an automatic out."

With his hit and 2 RBIs in his pocket, Hook continued to cruise on the mound that night.

"The pitchers developed a motto, or at least I did, and that was 'Don't give up a run because you'll lose the chance for a tie,'" Hook said with a hearty laugh.

When it was all said and done, Hook had given up only 1 run, scattered 5 hits, and pitched a complete game to lead the Mets to a 9–1 win—the franchise's first.

"It's fun," said Hook, reminiscing about the victory 50-plus years later. "You look back on something in your life and there's something that you always think about and that would have to be the thing. I still get maybe 10 letters a month with baseball cards in them."

One of the most impressive parts of the victory for Hook, as he looks back, was that he pitched a complete game—although that was nothing particularly special or unique for his time. In fact, in 1962 Hook had 13 complete games. In 2015, when the Mets won the National League pennant, only Bartolo Colón pitched a complete game. In fact, in 2015, no *team* in the major leagues had more than 11 complete games. The 1962 Mets—the worst team in baseball history—had 43 complete games.

"Baseball has certainly changed," Hook said. "Now, if a guy goes six innings they think he's had a quality start, but back then if we didn't complete games you would go to negotiate your contract and the general manager would say, 'Well, you only completed 12 games' or something like that. It was definitely looked at as a negative if you didn't complete games."

The Mets' celebratory ways that night would be short-lived. The team went on to lose seven of its next nine games and, as all Mets fans know, lost 120 games that first season.

Fans, despite their enthusiasm and excitement to have a National League team back in New York, were given a small dose in 1962—albeit extreme—of what it would mean at times to be a Mets fan. Never, however, have those fans wavered.

When the Mets have been down, their fans have been there with them—there to cry, there to understand, and there to support. That's not to say there hasn't been some frustration and anger at times—from 1962 to 1968, for example, or from 1974 to 1983, or from 1989 to 1998, or in 2017—well, you get the idea. However, through it all, Mets fans have remained true to the Blue and Orange. Perhaps that is why the good times have been so sweet.

Now, well into the sixth decade of their existence, the Mets have had more than their share of memorable moments—both during the regular season and in the postseason. There have been huge home runs, great pitching performances, All-Star excellence, key acquisitions, pennants, world championships, and yes, even a no-hitter!

For this book, we have selected 31 of the greatest moments in team history—a pretty significant number for the Mets. These moments will span the franchise's history—from the night that Hook pitched his complete game to lead the team to its very first victory.

As Hook explained it, one of his 13 grandchildren, who now lives and works in New York City, probably summed it up best: "She told me, 'I'm here in New York, and I'm a Mets fan, and to think you pitched the first game the Mets ever won. You gave us a great tradition.'"

One win down, one moment down, with many more to come, within—and beyond—this book.

2

Seaver's Nearly Perfect (1969)

There are few moments in franchise history in which time seems to stand still. However, on July 9, 1969, that is exactly what it felt like at Shea Stadium. Time had stopped, and Tom Seaver was controlling everything. He was controlling the record-59,083 fans in attendance on that Wednesday night, he was controlling the pace of the game—which moved as swiftly as any that season—and, more importantly, he was controlling the first-place Chicago Cubs—completely and absolutely.

Heading into the 1969 season, the Mets were not expected to be much of a force in the National League's Eastern Division. In 1968, they had finished with a 73-89 record under new manager Gil Hodges, which was good enough for ninth place in the National League. Only the Houston Astros were worse—and just one game worse—than the Mets. One of the lone bright spots for the 1968 Mets was Seaver, who in only his second season in the major leagues won 16 games, just as he had done as the 1967 Rookie of the Year.

By 1969, things had changed in the National League, as two new organizations entered—the Montreal Expos and San Diego Padres—and the league was split into two six-team divisions. The same happened in the American League, with the Seattle Pilots and Kansas City Royals being added. At the end of the regular season, there would now be a National League and American League Championship Series, during which the team finishing in first place in the Eastern and Western Divisions would play a best-of-five series to determine who would advance to the World Series.

Still, even with this new format, the Mets were not expected to do much of anything that year. The newly formed National League East included the St. Louis Cardinals, who had won 97 games in 1968. Other division mates were the Chicago Cubs, who had won 84 games, followed by the Pittsburgh Pirates, Philadelphia Phillies, and the expansion Expos. Other than perhaps the Expos, everyone had a better chance of winning the National League East than the Mets. They had never, after all, had a winning season. However, that—as they say—is why they play the games. And, as it turned out, the 1969 Mets were not the 1968 Mets.

After an uneven start to the season, the Mets really started to get on a consistent winning track heading into July. As Seaver took the mound on that July 9 night, the Mets were riding a six-game winning streak and were coming off of a walk-off win against the first-place Cubs the day before. The Cubs were sputtering and the Mets had to sense it. On July 3rd, Chicago had been ahead of the Mets by 8 games. If Seaver and the Mets could pull off another win, they would be able to close that gap to just 3½ games.

The scene was set, and the stage was Seaver's. To say he put on a good show would be the greatest of understatements.

"I am fortunate enough to have been at Shea Stadium to see the Mets win the division, the pennant, and the World Series, but my most memorable night in that ballpark was July 9, 1969," said Mets radio broadcaster Howie Rose. "It was the first series with pennant implications that the Mets had ever played, and the build-up to it was just enormous."

Seaver, who entered the game with 13 victories, would be facing Chicago's Ken Holtzman, who had 10 wins. Seaver was at his absolute best that night against the Cubs, breezing through the first three innings, striking out six of the nine batters he faced. Over the next three innings, the Cubs fared no better, as Seaver faced the minimum number of hitters. Again, in the seventh and eighth innings, Seaver was perfect.

Mets pitcher Jerry Koosman, who had pitched the day before for the Mets, refused to look in Seaver's direction.

"Certainly when you have a no-hitter going or a perfect game you don't talk to the pitcher because you don't want to jinx anything," Koosman said.

In the bottom of the eighth inning, Seaver came to bat with one on and one out, knowing in a few minutes that he was going to return to the mound to try to complete the perfect night. As he approached home plate for that at-bat, Mets fans let loose.

"If there is any one moment I relish from all the years at Shea Stadium it was the ovation—and I can put myself into the story—that *we* gave Tom when he came to bat in the bottom of the eighth inning," Rose said. "It was the most thunderous, meaningful ovation I'd ever heard or taken part in in my life. It wasn't just that he had a perfect game going; as he walked from the on-deck circle to home plate, the cheers and the ovation had as much to do with the realization that the Mets had arrived, that this was not only a good young pitcher but a transcendent player, and he was ours. If we were going to get there, he was going to be the guy to get us there. When you realize for the first time that the joke's over, that's a very, very profound feeling, and that was all encapsulated in that ovation. Being a part of that—and what it meant—is my single greatest memory in that ballpark. That was the night the Mets grew up."

Tom Seaver flirted with perfection on that memorable July night in 1969.

In the top of the ninth inning, Seaver got Cubs catcher Randy Hundley to bunt back to the mound for the first out. The next batter was rookie center fielder Jimmy Qualls, the number-eight hitter. As it turns out, Qualls would not have much of a major-league career. He ended up playing only 43 games for the Cubs in 1969 and just 63 games during his entire career. He was not necessarily a player who would be remembered by Cubs fans, or Expos or White Sox fans for that matter (nine games and 11 games played, respectively). He will, however, forever be known to Mets fans—and, of course, to Tom Seaver.

Qualls singled to center field, ending Seaver's bid at perfection and stunning an exuberant crowd at Shea Stadium. And while the pitcher himself took losing the perfect game in stride, his batterymate felt like the Mets ace was going to do something special.

"I thought it was going to be a no-hitter from the very first pitch," Mets catcher Jerry Grote told reporters following the game. "I think it's great if you always go out there with an attitude that it's going to be a perfect game."

For Koosman, it was certainly a disappointment to come that close, only to lose the perfect game in the ninth inning.

"When Qualls got that base hit, it was a letdown because I was rooting for my teammate," Koosman said, "and a perfect game would have been beautiful."

For his part, Qualls tried to remain out of the spotlight that he put himself in by doing the simplest of offensive tasks—getting a base hit. He was booed ferociously by Mets fans the following day, but the seldom-used player took it all in stride.

"The booing didn't bother me at all," the twenty-two-year-old outfielder told reporters after the game. "I know the New York fans wanted to see a perfect game, but I was glad I got the hit. The only thing I was sorry about was that we lost the game."

Nearly 20 years later, in 1988, Qualls remained matter-of-fact speaking about his role in Seaver's near perfection.

"That's what people remember me for, getting that hit off Tom Seaver," Qualls told the Associated Press. "I don't think they'd know me without that. I got a lot of letters from Mets fans that season. Some of them said nasty things. I still get one or two letters a week, mostly asking for autographs. But I haven't heard from any Mets fans for a while."

Forty years after losing his perfect game, in 2009, Seaver spoke to Richard Sandomir of the *New York Times* about what he remembered about that night.

"I felt like I was levitating," Seaver said. "I felt like I was coming off the ground. Talk about being scary. You think you're in control, but your body is saying, 'Oh no, you're not.'"

While Qualls's hit may have ended Seaver's perfect game, the 1969 Mets were just getting started for what was going to be the most memorable baseball season ever for the team and its fans.

3

Seaver Strikes Out 19 (1970)

From 1967 through the middle of the 1977 season, the Mets had one of the most exciting and talented players in all of baseball in Tom Seaver. Unfortunately, for far too many of those seasons, the Mets were not one of the top teams in the league. Therefore, for many of Tom Terrific's starts, there were far fewer fans on hand than Seaver deserved. April 22, 1970, was no exception. On that day, the defending world champions had just over 14 thousand fans go through the turnstiles at Shea Stadium to watch Seaver pitch. As painful as that might have seemed, there were nearly double the number of fans on hand for the game the day before.

The day started as a great one for Seaver, who received his 1969 Cy Young Award before the game began. Many of the fans on hand for the Wednesday afternoon game were students, as often was the case for mid-week day games.

It was the first Earth Day ever recognized, which was perfect for Seaver, who was holding the whole world in his hands on this day. Well, he was at the very least holding the San Diego Padres in his hand—his right hand.

From the very first inning, Seaver showed his dominance. After getting José Arcia to fly out to center field on the game's very first pitch, Seaver struck out Van Kelly and Cito Gaston. In the bottom of the first inning, the Mets scored when Ken Boswell doubled home Bud Harrelson.

In the top of the second inning, Seaver made his one and only mistake in the game, allowing a game-tying home run to the Padres' Al Ferrara. He struck out Jerry Morales to end the inning. Three strikeouts through two innings—not worth taking notice just yet.

Seaver then went on to strike out two more batters in the third (5 in three innings) and two more in the fourth (7 in four innings). In the top of the fifth inning, Tom Terrific fanned Bob Barton and Mike Corkins (9 in five innings) and struck out Al Ferrara to end the sixth inning (10 in six innings). However, that is when things got very interesting for Seaver and the Mets. The reason for that is that Seaver would not record another out in any manner other than the strikeout. Over the next three innings Seaver struck out Nate Colbert, Dave Campbell, Jerry Morales, Bob Barton, pinch-hitter Ramón Webster, pinch-hitter Ivan Murrell, Kelly, Gaston, and Al Ferrara. Lose count? Tom Seaver struck out the final 10 batters of the game for a then-record 19 strikeouts in the contest. No pitcher in baseball history—before or after 1970—has ever struck out 10-straight batters.

"I knew I was going to get the heat," the Brooklyn-born Ferrara told reporters after the game, "because he was really bringing it. . . . He got into a groove. He couldn't wait to get that ball and throw it at us. The guy deserved all the credit in the world because he was rushing it up there. He was about as fast as I've ever seen."

Over the final five innings, only three San Diego batters made contact with a Seaver pitch, and in the ninth inning he needed only 10 pitches to strike out the side.

"I might as well have played without a glove," shortstop Bud Harrelson said after the game.

Seaver admitted he was aware of what he was accomplishing as he was doing it.

"After I got the 16th strikeout," Seaver told reporters after the game, "I thought about Steve Carlton striking out 19 against us last year and losing the game, 4–3. We only had a one-run lead, and I knew I had to pitch to Ferrara in the ninth. I kept that thought until I got two strikes on Ferrara. Then I thought, *What the heck. I may never come this close again. I might as well go for it.*"

The Mets' ace also made note following the game that neither he nor the crowd at Shea was as emotional about the feat as when he lost his perfect game against the Cubs the previous season.

Tom Seaver's performance against the San Diego Padres was one for the ages.

"The commotion wasn't as great," he told reporters. "You have to remember this was an expansion club and the Cubs were leading the league, and there were 59 thousand people here for that game. . . . I'm very happy about it. But 19 strikeouts doesn't exhilarate me as much as a perfect game."

4

Say Hey's Big Comeback (1972)

"Willie, Mickey, and the Duke" means different things to different New York baseball fans, depending on team allegiance. Three New York baseball teams with three star center fielders, all playing in the same town at the same time—the best of baseball writers could not make up a better story.

Of course, Mickey Mantle is arguably the greatest and most popular New York Yankee to ever live. He was named the American League's Most Valuable Player three times, was a 20-time All-Star—yes, 20-time All Star—and won the Triple Crown in 1956. Oh, and by the way, he led his team to a world championship seven times. He was voted into the Hall of Fame in 1974.

Duke Snider, meanwhile, played for the Brooklyn Dodgers and was an eight-time All-Star. He led Brooklyn to its only world championship in 1955 over the mighty Yankees and was also part of the Los Angeles Dodgers team that won the World Series in 1959, but that of course doesn't count in terms of the New York discussion. He was inducted into the Hall of Fame in 1980.

Then, there was Willie Mays, who patrolled the cavernous center field at the Polo Grounds for the New York Giants. His over-the-shoulder catch against Cleveland's Vic Wertz during the 1954 World Series is one of the most well-known baseball highlights that exists. Giants radio announcer Jack Brickhouse made the historic call:

There's a long drive, waaaay back in center field, way back, back, it is—oh, caught by Willie Mays . . . Willie Mays just brought this crowd to its feet . . . with a catch . . . which must have been an optical illusion to a lot of people. Boy!

When the Giants followed the Dodgers to California after the 1957 season, Snider and Mays were suddenly gone, as was National League baseball. New Yorkers who chose not to root for the Yankees—National League fans—had to endure three seasons with no baseball in New York. Of course, that all changed in 1962 when the New York Mets came along.

One year later, in an attempt to recapture some of those good ol' days, the Mets brought an aging Duke Snider back to New York for one last season in the city that he was so much a part of. The thirty-six-year-old's 14 home runs gave Brooklyn Dodgers fans one last hurrah with their favorite son, but that was about all. The '63 Mets were less lovable than the '62 Mets and certainly less lovable than Snider's old Brooklyn Bums.

Ten years after the Mets were born, another well-past-his-prime superstar returned to New York. However, it didn't seem to matter how old Willie Mays was, or that he had lost more than a few steps. He was Willie Mays, the "Say Hey Kid," and he was once again going to be wearing an interlocking NY on his baseball cap. He had worn a similar cap—a black one with the same interlocking NY—during his seven years with the New York Giants. And while Mays may have lost those steps, apparently he hadn't lost his flair for the dramatic.

In his first game as a member of the Mets, 35,505 fans packed into Shea Stadium on a rainy Sunday to see the legend's debut as a home player in Flushing against—who else—the San Francisco Giants, the team that had traded Mays to the Mets three days earlier. Mays had certainly done his job in San Francisco. Over his 14-plus seasons in the Bay Area, Mays was a 14-time All-Star and 11-time Gold Glove Award winner. In 1965, Mays's best year as a San Francisco Giant, he slugged 52 home runs, led the National League in six offensive categories, and was named the league's Most Valuable Player.

However, by 1972, the forty-one-year-old Mays was breaking down, the Giants were losing money, and there didn't seem to be a future in San Francisco in any capacity for the future Hall of Famer. Plus, Mays was unhappy that the Giants were not using him in lieu of younger players. Mays reportedly wanted certain guarantees that he would have a job with the Giants beyond his playing days, but the Giants were not in a position to make any such guarantees and decided to trade Mays to the Mets. In New York, Mays would have more opportunities after baseball, as the Mets agreed to make him a coach for at least three seasons after he retired. He was traded in May for Charlie Williams and $50,000.

Mays was excited about his return to the city where his major-league career started.

"It's a wonderful feeling," Mays told reporters after the trade was completed, "and I'm very thankful I can come back to New York. I don't think I'm just on display here. There's no doubt in my mind that I can help the Mets if I'm used in the right way."

In the bottom of the fifth inning of his first game, Mays started to help the Mets when he blasted a 3–2 pitch from reliever Don Carrithers for a home run—the 647th of his career.

Mets broadcaster Lindsey Nelson described the home run this way on the radio:

> Payoff pitch to Mays—and it's way back in left field, it could be, it's going, going, and it is a home run! A home run for Willie Mays! Number six hundred forty-seven in his career.

Willie Mays homers in his very first game wearing a Mets uniform.

After Mays rounded the bases, Nelson described the standing ovation Mays received for the homer, which put the Mets up 5–4.

Following the game, Mays met with reporters and admitted that he had mixed feelings in his first game with the Mets.

"It was a strange feeling to bat against a team I played 21 years for," Mays said. "When you play for a club and do something against them you always have to have some feeling. I wanted to help the Mets, but I had some feeling for the Giants, too."

For Mets rookie pitcher Jon Matlack, having Mays on the team in 1972 meant a tremendous amount:

> It was a really neat experience and a very valuable experience as well. He might have been toward the end of his playing days as far as his physical attributes were concerned, but there was nothing wrong with his instincts or mental attributes that he brought to the ballgame. There was a lot that could be learned from his knowledge of the game and way he played the game.

That home run would not be the last hurrah for Mays, however. Mays finished out the 1972 season with the Mets and returned for the 1973 season. He was the elder statesman for the National League Championship team, which took the Oakland Athletics to Game Seven of the World Series. Mays retired following the 1973 season, with a career batting average of .302, 660 home runs, and 338 stolen bases. He was a 24-time All Star, recorded more outfield putouts than anyone else who played the game, and was inducted into the Hall of Fame in 1979.

Matlack acknowledges that being a teammate of Mays was something he will always remember.

"I was tickled to death to be a part of that," Matlack said. "I have a picture in a frame of a postgame congratulatory handshake between he and I. He had played first base, and we were walking off the field, and someone took a picture of us shaking hands. And it's still one of my prized possessions sitting on my desk at home."

5

Maz Is a Midsummer Star (1979)

It is saying something to proclaim that 1979 was possibly the worst season the Mets had endured. Sure, there was the 1962 campaign during which the Mets lost 120 games—but that team was brand new and lovable. In 1979, the team was just depressing. Only 788,905 fans showed up to watch the Mets that year at Shea Stadium, which was—although only 15 years old—literally falling apart.

"Nothing was more depressing than seeing that ballpark and seeing that team in 1979," said Mets broadcaster Howie Rose. "I know there were worse seasons, but to me that was the low point in the history of the franchise. New York City was broke, Shea Stadium was a municipal building, and it was in ridiculous disrepair for a place that was only 15 years old. To see the way it looked in 1979 was tremendously depressing. It just hurt. Knowing what the Mets had meant to this town and what that ballpark was like in the late '60s and early '70s—when the Mets absolutely owned New York—it was really painful."

Some of the few bright spots for the Mets and their fans were players such as Brooklyn-born Lee Mazzilli. With his matinee-idol looks, Mazzilli—who appeared as though he belonged on the set of the film *Saturday Night Fever*—was having his best season with the Mets in what was only his third full year in the majors. At the All-Star break, Mazzilli was hitting .320 with 9 home runs and 48 runs batted in. When it came time to select the National League squad, manager Tommy Lasorda actually chose two Mets—Mazzilli and hard-nosed catcher John Stearns, who had been an All-Star in 1977 as well.

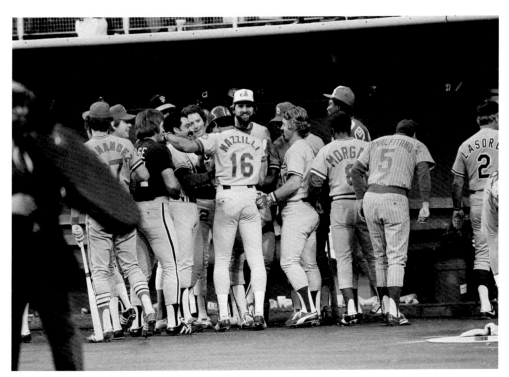

Lee Mazzilli is greeted by his National League teammates after hitting a game-tying home run.

While Stearns never made it into the game—the only All-Star Game ever played at Seattle's Kingdome—Mazzilli was called upon to be a pinch-hitter in the top of the eighth inning with the National League trailing 6–5. Facing Texas Rangers pitcher Jim Kern, Mazzilli—batting lefty—slashed an opposite-field home run down the left-field line to tie the game. It was the first-ever pinch-hit home run in all-star history.

"I knew Kern threw hard, but I had never faced him before, so I really didn't have any idea of what kind of stuff he had," Mazzilli later told Mets broadcasters. "I was just looking for a fastball knowing that he threw hard. He fell behind me and threw a fastball that I hit 317½ feet and it's only 317 down the line. I hit the ball well, and I didn't really know it was out until I got between first and second base, and I was just overjoyed about it."

One inning later, Mazzilli, who had stayed in the game and was playing center field, got another chance to be an all-star hero. However, it would not be against Kern, who was pulled from the game after walking the bases loaded.

"I knew," Mazzilli told reporters after the game, "that if they walked Ron Cey ahead of me, [Ron] Guidry would come in. The only time I faced him was in spring training. He's one of the best pitchers in baseball. It was like the battle of New York."

Mazzilli was exactly right. American League manager Bob Lemon—who also happened to be Guidry's manager with the Yankees—went to the pen for the man they called "Louisiana Lightning." Mazzilli and Guidry, it seemed, traveled more than 2,862 miles to face each other. Yankee Stadium was just 9.7 miles from Shea Stadium, by the way.

Despite not knowing Guidry all that well, Mazzilli knew one thing—he was going to get heat.

"What was I looking for? Fastball, slider, something hard," Mazzilli said, when questioned by reporters after the game. "He threw a fastball on the first pitch, and it wasn't around the plate at all. The 2–0 pitch I hit foul past third base, that was a ball really. He was high all night."

Guidry went on to walk Mazzilli, who was credited with the game-winning run batted in, as the National League held on for a 7–6 victory. Had it not been for the arm of Dave Parker—who unleashed an incredible throw to gun down a runner trying to score in the bottom of the eighth inning—Mazzilli most definitely would have been the game's Most Valuable Player. That honor instead went to Parker.

Instead, Mazzilli had to settle for having the time of his life in what would be his only trip to an All-Star Game during his 14-year major league career.

Years later, when interviewed by ESPN's Mark Simon, Mazzilli looked back fondly on his only midsummer classic.

"I was just hoping I wouldn't embarrass myself," he said. "How do you describe something where you are completely overtaken by the experience? It was one of the greatest experiences of my career. For one day, you're the best in the world."

6

The Franchise Returns (1983)

As Tom Seaver walked out to the mound at Shea for his start on a sunny Sunday afternoon in August, all the fans took notice. That mound at Shea had belonged to Seaver for the past 10 years—and was the platform from which he had orchestrated some of his greatest masterpieces. He had won the National League Rookie of the Year, three Cy Young Awards, two National League pennants, and one world championship—all from that mound. He had come close to pitching a perfect game—and had struck out 19 Padres in a single game—all from that mound.

On this day in 1977, however, Seaver took a different route to the mound. He didn't take his usual path from the Mets dugout to the center of the diamond. Instead, he approached the mound from the other direction—from the visitor's dugout. More than two months after being traded by the Mets to the Reds—front-page news in the *New York Times* that devastated Mets Nation—Seaver was about to face his former team for the very first time. While more than 46 thousand fans looked on, Seaver pitched the Reds past his former team, 5–1.

"The toughest part was waiting for the game to start," Seaver told reporters following the game. "Once it got going, I was all right. I said it was not emotional, but that was just to keep everything inside. You have to do that. You have to discipline your mind. You have to go out and be professional. I'd be lying if I said it wasn't an emotional game."

After spending nearly 10 seasons as the Mets ace, Seaver spent the remainder of the 1977 season, as well as 1978 through 1982, with the Reds. He enjoyed good seasons in Cincinnati, but the Reds could not maintain the momentum they had earlier in the 1970s and reached the postseason only once with Seaver on the team, losing to the Pittsburgh Pirates in the NLCS in 1979.

By 1982, the Reds were a last-place team, losing more than 100 games. The years had taken their toll on Seaver, as well, who struggled through an injury-plagued 5–13 season. With Seaver's contract expiring at the end of the 1983 season, Cincinnati decided to move the future Hall of Famer. In December of 1982, Seaver was traded back to the Mets in exchange for Lloyd McClendon, Charlie Puleo, and a minor leaguer. The Franchise was back.

"I let it be known that I was interested in going back home," Seaver told reporters at the time. "I was a 10/5 man (10-year veteran, five with the same team) and could ask to be traded. That year, I had a sore arm; I really didn't pitch the last half of the year. I felt I could still pitch, but if I was not in Cincinnati's plans, I would've preferred to go back to New York."

The stage was now set. Seaver's second act with the Mets would begin on Opening Day. Shea was packed to the rafters. On September 30, 1982, the final game of that season at Shea, only 5,293 fans passed through the turnstiles. On this day, the very next home game—separated by an offseason and a trade—46,687 fans stormed into the building.

As Seaver walked in from the Mets bullpen in right field before the game, the crowd went berserk. Seaver—clad once again in the royal blue pinstripes and a satin Mets jacket—waved at the crowd, tipped his cap, looked down at the ground, and walked past a dozen or so photographers on the field just in front of the Mets dugout.

"Walking in from the bullpen, at a place where I have so many beautiful memories, it was very touching," Seaver told Ralph Kiner on *Kiner's Korner* following the game.

After shaking hands with each of his teammates, Seaver emerged from the dugout for the start of the game. The Shea mound that had long been his home was there waiting.

When Seaver threw his first pitch to leadoff batter Pete Rose, he tied Walter Johnson's record of 14 opening-day starts. Seaver, who would go on to break that record in subsequent years, ended up striking out Rose to start the game. The crowd—already in a frenzy—exploded in joy.

Following the strikeout of Rose—who had struck out only 32 times in 634 at-bats in 1982—Mets broadcaster Ralph Kiner described the reaction:

So Tom Seaver, with a good breaking pitch, gets Pete Rose on a strike-out—something you don't see often. . . . Tom Seaver, with over 3,000 strikeouts in his career and 10 times he has struck out 200 or more batters, something no one else has ever done.

Seaver pitched well in his return to the Mets, throwing six innings of 3-hit ball. He struck out 5 and walked just 1. Unfortunately, the Mets could not muster any runs until Seaver had left the game, scoring twice in the bottom of the seventh inning. Rookie Doug Sisk entered the game and pitched three scoreless innings for the win.

"I knew it would be emotional," Seaver told reporters after the game, "but I didn't think it would be that emotional."

Despite not recording the victory, the day was one to remember for Seaver and for Mets fans.

"All I can say about Opening Day is that it was a perfect day," Seaver said after the game.

Tom Seaver delivers a pitch on Opening Day in 1983.

Seaver went on to win 9 games for the Mets in 1983. However, in a severe error in judgment, the team left Seaver unprotected in the 1983 free-agent compensation pool. The Mets had to protect 26 players and assumed that no other teams would be interested in the aging righty. They assumed wrong, and Seaver was gobbled up by the Chicago White Sox. Seaver was incensed and didn't hide his emotions at a press conference.

"The Mets certainly made a mistake by not protecting me," Seaver told the reporters gathered at Shea Stadium. "You don't have to be a Harvard Law student to figure that out. They admit it."

After considering retirement, Seaver instead went on to pitch for the White Sox, winning 15 games in 1984 and 16 more in 1985. The biggest of those wins came when Seaver defeated the New York Yankees to earn his 300th career victory. The Yankees' television station, WPIX, invited former Mets announcer Lindsey Nelson—who called games for the Mets from 1962 through 1978—into the booth to announce the bottom of the ninth inning. With two outs, Don Baylor stepped in to face Seaver:

> Seaver's ready to work now to Don Baylor—and it's a high fly ball that should be playable—Nichols is moving over, Nichols is there—the ball game is over! Seaver has won 300! He has become the 17th man in the history of baseball to win 300 games.

He capped his career by splitting the 1986 season with the White Sox and Boston Red Sox. In fact, Seaver was in the dugout as a member of the Red Sox during the 1986 World Series. He was injured, however, and did not pitch in the Series.

The following season, Seaver made one last-ditch effort to return for one last season with the Mets. However, after attempting to get himself in playing shape for the Mets in 1987, the forty-two-year-old decided it was time to retire.

Joseph Durso wrote in the *New York Times*, "Seaver reached his decision after pitching four dull innings in a simulated game at Shea, a performance that he described as 'so-so and mediocre.' 'The bottom line is I'm not pleased with the way I'm throwing.'"

One year later, on June 24, 1988, Tom Seaver became the first Mets player to have his uniform number retired.

7

Doc's All-Star Spectacular (1984)

When the 1983 season ended for the Mets, there was reason for optimism for the future of the franchise. The Mets had acquired all-star first baseman Keith Hernandez, outfielder Darryl Strawberry was named the National League Rookie of the Year, and the Mets had one of the finest minor-league systems in all of baseball. Still, there was not much in the way of pitching on the team, and the 1983 squad finished 68–94, 22 games out of first place. The question was, how quickly could some of that minor-league talent get to Shea Stadium?

One of the top minor-league talents the Mets had was a pitcher by the name of Dwight Gooden, who was selected fifth overall by the Mets in the 1982 draft. In 1983, while the Mets were struggling to put solid pitching on the mound, Gooden dominated for Class A Lynchburg of the Carolina League. Sure, it was only Class A, but Gooden won 19 games and struck out 300—yes, 300—batters that season. Davey Johnson, who was the manager of the triple-A Tidewater Tides in 1983, was so impressed by Gooden that he called the eighteen-year-old righty up to his team for the Tides' postseason run. With Gooden getting some postseason experience with the Tides in 1983, the stage had been set—and Johnson became the show's director—when he was named as manager of the Mets before the 1984 season.

Gooden burst on the scene in 1984 with the Mets, mixing a blazing fastball with a curveball that was simply staggering. He was quickly given the nickname of "Dr. K" due to all the strikeouts he threw, and while in general a curveball was known as "Uncle Charlie" throughout baseball, Gooden's became known

Dwight Gooden took the National League by storm in 1984.

as "Lord Charles." Gooden was giving the Mets the impact player that they had lacked for so many years.

"It was immediate, and it was desperately needed because the Mets had been floundering for many years," said Mets broadcaster Howie Rose. "There really was very little sign of them turning the corner until 1984 came around and they had established a pretty good young pitching staff of which Doc was the centerpiece. It was so easy to see between the explosive fastball and knee-buckling curve that if this kid would stay healthy and with whatever little refinement that he needed he was going to be special. And he was special really from the first day he threw a baseball for the Mets. It was as exciting as it was electrifying, and it really made your mind jump around with all of the possibilities that existed."

That excitement reached a peak when Gooden, who went 8–5 during the first half of the season, was named the youngest All-Star ever. When he stepped on the mound during the 1984 All-Star Game in San Francisco, Gooden didn't disappoint. The nineteen-year-old struck out all three batters he faced in the top of the fifth inning—Lance Parrish and Chet Lemon of the Tigers and Alvin Davis of the Mariners—showing the world what the Mets now had in their arsenal.

"It reminded me very much of when Tom Seaver was a rookie in 1967 and he came on to get the last out of the All-Star Game," Rose said. "Even though the 1984 Mets were much, much better than the 1967 team, I got that same feeling of anticipation and pride. It sort of validated where the Mets were at that time, as they were in first place at the time and no one had seen them coming at the beginning of the year. To see Gooden basically grab the stage and make it his own, it really made your chest puff up and stick out as a fan, and you just get lost in the possibilities. You saw that and said, 'Oh my goodness, what in the world do we have here?'"

Mets pitching coach Mel Stottlemyre credited Gooden's makeup for much of his success. To go along with his incredible talent at such a young age, Gooden could stay focused on the big picture.

"The thing about Dwight is his poise," Stottlemyre told reporters during the summer of 1986. "He's not going to beat himself. Other young pitchers panic or lose control in tight situations. He'll never do that. Man on third, no out, he usually makes the big pitches. That's a very unusual trait."

If Mets fans were encouraged by Gooden's performance in the midsummer classic, they had to be downright giddy about what the pitcher was able to do in

September. Despite the fact that the Mets would fall short of the Chicago Cubs for the division title in 1984, Gooden showed everyone what he was all about.

On September 7 against those same Cubs, Gooden pitched a one-hit shutout, leading to a 10–0 Mets win. The only hit Gooden surrendered was an infield single to Keith Moreland in the fifth inning. He struck out 11 in the game to break Grover Cleveland Alexander's National League record for strikeouts by a rookie. Alexander had struck out 227 in 1911, and following the victory Gooden had 235.

Gooden seemed unfazed that he nearly pitched a no-hitter.

"I'm not disappointed," Gooden told reporters following the game. "The hit doesn't matter. I just wanted to win the game."

Five days later, Gooden was at it again, this time pitching a shutout against the Pittsburgh Pirates. Gooden struck out 16 batters in the game and walked no one. As he had in his last start, Gooden broke another rookie strikeout record. This time, he surpassed the record of 245 strikeouts set by Herb Score in 1955.

Gooden would go on to win 17 games in his Rookie of the Year campaign and struck out a league-leading 276 batters. It was the most strikeouts Gooden would ever have in a single season. It was the start of what appeared to be an elite career in the majors for Gooden and the Mets. Gooden went on to pitch one of the greatest seasons ever in 1985, going 24–4 with an earned run average of 1.53 and striking out a league-leading 268 batters. While Gooden would have a few more very good seasons for the Mets, the reality was that Gooden was never able to sustain the greatness and fulfill what the organization and fans thought he would become. Drug problems and injuries limited Gooden's greatness with the Mets, and by 1994, just 10 years after breaking into the big leagues, Gooden was gone. After missing the entire 1995 season, Gooden was signed in 1996 by the New York Yankees.

That season, and 12 years after bursting on the scene as the best young pitcher in baseball, thirty-one-year-old Dwight Gooden finally pitched a no-hitter—for the Yankees. Gooden shut down the Seattle Mariners for a 2–0 victory at Yankee Stadium, where he was carried off the field by his teammates. He was inducted into the Mets Hall of Fame in 2010.

8

The Kid Comes to Town (1985)

When Dwight Gooden struck out his third-straight batter in the 1984 All-Star Game, Montreal Expos catcher Gary Carter pumped his fist on the way to the National League dugout. It is doubtful that Carter was thinking anything other than, *Yes, we just struck out the side*, and maybe even, *Wow, this kid looks great*. However, he was most likely not thinking that he was going to be Gooden's catcher the following season.

"I can remember in the 1984 All-Star Game, when Gooden struck out the side, thinking not necessarily, *Wouldn't it be great if Gary Carter became the Mets catcher*, but, *Man, how great would it be to have a catcher of that magnitude to work with these young pitchers—and especially Doc*," said Mets broadcaster Howie Rose. "Of course, presto, a few months later there he was."

The 1984 Mets seemingly came out of nowhere, but, looking back, the pieces were being put in place. In 1983, the last-place Mets had a record of 68–94 and finished 22 games behind the first-place Philadelphia Phillies. Still, good things were happening. Young outfield prospect Darryl Strawberry arrived in the majors in early May and would go on to win the National League Rookie of the Year Award. Just over one month later, the Mets and Cardinals made a blockbuster trade, with the Mets acquiring Keith Hernandez, a five-time Gold Glove winner and 1979 Co-Most Valuable Player, in exchange for pitchers Neil Allen and Rick Ownbey. Suddenly, the Mets had gotten younger and stronger.

At the start of the 1984 season, nineteen-year-old Dwight Gooden made the big-league team and was considered one of the best young arms in all of baseball. Gooden, along with young pitchers such as Ron Darling, Walt Terrell, and Sid Fernandez, led the Mets to an impressive 90 victories that year and a surprise run at the National League East crown. While the Mets fell just short of going worst to first in 1984, finishing 6½ games behind the Chicago Cubs, they served notice that they were going to be a team to be reckoned with moving forward. They seemed to need one more piece.

That piece came on December 10, 1984, when Mets general manager Frank Cashen pulled off one of the biggest blockbuster trades in team history, sending Hubie Brooks, Mike Fitzgerald, Herm Winningham, and Floyd Youmans to the Expos in exchange for Carter, the seven-time all-star catcher. The Expos had been unable to accommodate Carter's escalating salary demands and decided to get as many young players as they could for the superstar.

Perhaps most importantly for the Mets, Carter really wanted to play for New York.

"I could've vetoed the trade if I'd wanted to," Carter told reporters after the deal was announced. "One of the reasons I didn't was that I was aware of the fine nucleus of young talent on the Mets. They're a fine team that just missed winning the division last year."

For the Mets, Carter was the final piece of the puzzle—a veteran catcher to lead a young, extremely talented pitching staff.

"When you have a young pitching staff as talented as that Mets staff was, you really would benefit greatly from not only a veteran catcher but a star

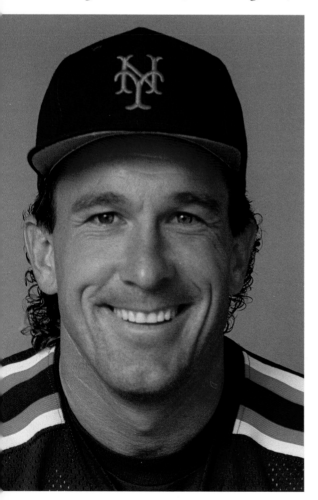

When the Mets traded for Gary Carter prior to the 1985 season, all of the pieces were in place for a championship run.

that not only knew the pitchers but knew the psychology of pitching and understood the game the way that Gary did," Rose said.

On the field, Carter provided what pitchers like Gooden, Darling, and the others needed at that point of their careers.

"It had to be a huge help to them because he was an accomplished veteran who knew the league and knew situations and had been with good teams," Rose said. "Gary was at a point in his career where he could take a pitching staff and make it better."

However, Carter was more than simply a great veteran catcher brought in to tutor young pitchers; he was a bona fide offensive force. Between 1977 and 1984, Carter averaged 24 home runs and 85 runs batted in per season.

Carter wasted little time enamoring himself to his new teammates and to Mets fans. On Opening Day of 1985, the Mets needed their newest star to come up big at a crucial moment, and he did not disappoint. With the game tied 5–5 and one out in the bottom of the 10th inning, Carter stepped up to the plate against Neil Allen, one of the pitchers sent to the Cardinals when the Mets traded for Keith Hernandez. Mets radio announcer Bob Murphy described the action, as Carter ripped into one of Allen's curveballs:

> Well-hit, deep to left field, way back, it may go, it is—at the top of the wall—gone, a home run, a home run. Gary Carter wins it.

"Welcome to New York, Gary Carter," Mets television announcer Steve Zabriskie added.

The acquisition of Carter meant everything for the Mets, and that was not lost on his new teammates. Just three days before Carter was traded to the Mets, a young infielder by the name of Howard Johnson was traded to New York from the Detroit Tigers in exchange for pitcher Walt Terrell.

"I was a National League fan for most of my life growing up, and I always knew that Gary was one of the best catchers in baseball, period," Johnson said. "Getting him was the icing on the cake. Game. Set. Match. We didn't win in '85, but we came close. And that set the stage for '86. We added a couple of more pieces, and it was just a matter of us playing the way we were capable of playing. Gary just kind of brought that winning mentality. He was a veteran and knew how to handle our pitching staff, and there were no issues when he was behind the plate. He was in command."

Carter would go on to have a Hall of Fame career, including 11 all-star appearances, three Gold Glove Awards, and five Silver Slugger Awards as the best hitting catcher in the game. He was inducted into the Mets Hall of Fame in 2001 and two years later received baseball's highest honor when Cooperstown called. On February 16, 2012, Carter died at the age of 57 of brain cancer. Four days later, the Montreal Canadiens paid tribute to Carter by all wearing number-eight jerseys during their pregame warm-up skate. They wore the number eight on their helmets for the remainder of the 2012 season. When the 2012 baseball season began, the Mets wore a patch on their jerseys that featured a black home plate, with the number eight and "KID" inscribed on it. On Opening Day, the Carter family unveiled a banner with a similar design on the center-field wall of Citi Field that remained for the 2012 season.

Although they won 98 games, the Mets indeed would fall just a little short in 1985, 3 games behind the Cardinals. However, thanks to an ever-improving pitching staff, as well as offensive players such as Hernandez, Strawberry, and Carter, the stage was now fully set.

9

An Interleague Stunner (1997)

It was a chant that Mets players had heard thousands of times per season—"Let's go Mets! Let's go Mets! The encouraging cheer reverberated throughout the stadium, from foul line to foul line, from the field level to the upper deck—*"Let's go Mets! Let's go Mets!"* With each big out the Mets got, the crowd roared with approval. There was just one thing that was different about these cheers the Mets were hearing—they were being shouted in the Bronx.

"When there was a strike three, they'd roar like we were at Shea," Mets infielder Matt Franco told reporters after the game. Mets starting pitcher Dave Mlicki told reporters that he had pitched in front of big crowds before, but "never a New York crowd like this."

★ ★ ★

The 1996 season did not go well for the Mets—in any way, shape, or form. The team won just 71 games that season and finished 25 games behind the division-winning Atlanta Braves. Other than Todd Hundley and Bernard Gilkey—each of whom had terrific offensive campaigns—the season was a total loss. To make matters worse for Mets fans, across town the Yankees were the toast of baseball. Led by American League Rookie of the Year Derek Jeter and an assortment of veteran stars, the Yankees won their first world championship since 1978. It was a tough time to be a Mets fan.

Heading into the 1997 season, there was little reason to believe the fortunes of either team would change. The Yankees appeared to be on the way up, and the Mets did not. However, there was something about the 1997 schedule that was different—and most definitely intriguing. On Monday, June 16, the Mets opponent was going to be the Yankees in a game that would actually count. That had never happened before. Prior to 1997, the Mets and Yankees had only met either

Pitcher Dave Mlicki will forever be remembered by Mets fans for defeating the Yankees in the first-ever interleague game.

in spring training or in the annual Mayor's Trophy Game, a New York tradition that dated back to the 1940s when the Yankees, New York Giants, and Brooklyn Dodgers used to play an in-season exhibition game. Beginning in 1963, the Mets and Yankees resumed the tradition and continued to play for the next 20 years. Due to a lack of interest, however, the exhibition game was eliminated from the schedule after 1983.

Fourteen years later, Major League Baseball instituted Interleague Play—and the Mets and Yankees would meet three times, with all games played at Yankee Stadium. Surprisingly, the two teams had very similar records heading into the first Subway Series—as it had been dubbed, throwing back to the vintage days of baseball when two New York teams would meet in the World Series. The Yankees entered with a 37–29 record and the Mets stood at 36–30. The three games would do little to alter the National or American League standings, but they would allow one of the two teams to have bragging rights. That was something important to the fans of both teams—and, of course, Yankees owner George Steinbrenner, who disliked losing to the Mets even in spring training.

"It's well documented that these games are important to our owner," Yankees pitcher David Cone told reporters before the series began, "as they should be. It's for the bragging rights of New York City."

Perhaps no one summed up the Subway Series better than writer Murray Chass—one of the finest-ever baseball writers—who wrote in the *New York Times* after Game One: "Forget the Mayor's Trophy Game, forget Fort Lauderdale, forget St. Petersburg. This was New York, and this was for real."

Real indeed—especially for twenty-nine-year-old Dave Mlicki, who was the starting pitcher for the Mets in Game One and understood what was at stake.

"I took a walk out to Monument Park before the game, just to try and get a sense of the stadium, and I tell you, I got goosebumps," Mlicki said. "When the schedule came out before the season started, that was a date I circled that I wanted to pitch."

Mlicki certainly pitched that night, baffling the defending world champions for nine innings, giving up no runs on 9 hits, while striking out 9. His final strikeout came on the last out of the game, as Mlicki fooled Derek Jeter with a curveball for a called strike three to cap off the 6–0 shutout. The fans remaining in the ballpark erupted in cheers. Mlicki gave a quick hug and flashed a big smile to his battery mate, Todd Hundley, and then turned around and exhaled. He had just won the biggest game of his career.

"Everything was working for me that night," Mlicki said during a Mets telecast in 2017. "I had a really good curveball that I remember, and I got a lot of guys swinging and looking at that. Pitching is never easy, but if you are hitting your spots and you have four pitches working it sure makes it a lot more fun."

The Mets would go on to lose the next two games to the Yankees, but the fact is, no one remembers that. More than 20 years later, however, fans still reflect on how Mlicki and the Mets went into the Bronx that night and beat the defending champion Yankees. For the Mets, it meant bragging rights for one night. For Mlicki, however, it meant bragging rights forever.

"We were absolutely the underdog and really weren't supposed to do anything. They were the defending champs," Mlicki said. "At the time, I knew that it was big, but I didn't know how big. In fact, it didn't hit me until days later, and it was such a cool feeling. It was just awesome."

10

Mets Get Piazza Delivery (1998)

It was raining at Citi Field leading up to the pregame ceremony on Saturday, July 30, 2016. The Mets were getting set to take on the Colorado Rockies in the second game of a three-game series, yet not even one of the 42,207 people in attendance cared. All of the fans had arrived early, despite the weather. Historical events tend to get people to the stadium on time, after all. It was during the pregame ceremony on this day that Mike Piazza was having his number 31 retired by the Mets. One week earlier, on a blazing hot afternoon in Cooperstown, New York, Piazza had been enshrined in the National Baseball Hall of Fame in front of an estimated crowd of 50 thousand screaming fans. Now, on this night in Flushing, it was more of a family thing.

As Piazza stepped out of the Mets dugout and onto the tarp, making his way out to the podium set up in short center field, the crowd exploded in cheers. It was a complete celebration of Mike Piazza and everything he had meant to—and means to—Mets fans.

It seems impossible to think that this wasn't always the case.

"Mike is revered now, but there were some pretty rough days between late May of 1998 and mid-August," said Mets broadcaster Howie Rose. "He was struggling, and it was getting to him. He was getting booed, which a lot of people might not remember."

When the 1998 season opened up, there was no thought that the Mets would be able to add a player such as Mike Piazza to their roster. There was really no reason to believe that Piazza was ever going to leave Los Angeles. After all, he had gone from being a 62nd-round draft pick in 1988 to one of the greatest-hitting catchers to ever put on a uniform.

In 1997, Piazza had a batting average of .362, slammed 40 homers, and drove in 124 runs—his best season in the majors in every one of those categories. He was the face of the Dodgers, a true superstar, and the most unlikely player in the majors to be traded. However, as the 1998 season began, Piazza was reportedly unhappy with the way contract negotiations with the Dodgers were going. Prior to the 1997 season, Piazza and his agent had asked for a six-year, $60 million contract extension but were turned down. They instead accepted arbitration and agreed to a two-year, $15 million deal that left Piazza less than thrilled. The team was in the process of being sold to Fox, and Piazza realized that he didn't seem to be a priority. The Dodgers offered him a six-year, $80 million contract just before the start of the 1998 season, which Piazza refused. Los Angeles was afraid that they would lose the slugger at the end of season and decided to be proactive.

On May 14, the deal was made. The 1993 National League Rookie of the Year and five-time All-Star was traded with veteran Todd Zeile to the Florida Marlins for Gary Sheffield, Bobby Bonilla, Charles Johnson, Jim Eisenreich, and minor leaguer Manuel Barrios. Dodger fans were stunned—and angry.

It quickly was obvious, however, that the Marlins acquired the twenty-nine-year-old Piazza in order to dump some of their own salaries and would soon be flipping Piazza as well. The question was, where would Piazza end up?

It seemed, at least for a while, that it would be the Chicago Cubs. However, the Cubs refused to part with their top catching prospect, Pat Cline, and their top pitching prospect, Todd Noel. Looking back, that turned out to be a little short-sighted on the part of the Cubs, as neither man would ever reach the majors.

The Mets, it seemed, were not serious contenders for the star catcher.

"I don't see a fit for us," Mets general manager Steve Phillips told the media. "For me to give up chips to get a player for the rest of this year who duplicates—when healthy—one of our strengths, it really doesn't make sense to do anything like that. We've got arguably one of the top three catchers in baseball ourselves."

Still, Todd Hundley was not Mike Piazza. At the end of the day, it was just too good to pass up, and just eight days after being traded to the Marlins, Piazza was sent to the Mets in exchange for Preston Wilson, Ed Yarnall, and minor leaguer Geoff Goetz.

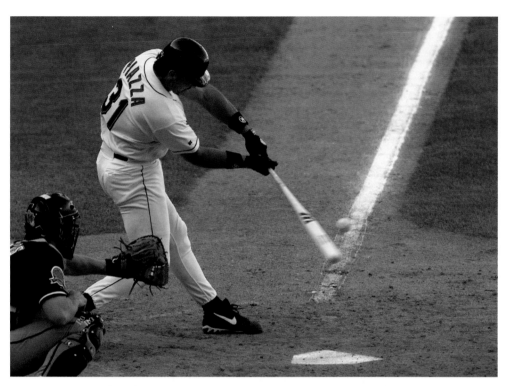

Mike Piazza strokes his first hit as a member of the Mets.

"I'm ecstatic to be able to acquire an offensive force that instantly adds credibility to our lineup," Phillips said when he announced the trade.

After all the speculation, all the buzz, all the denials, Piazza was a member of the Mets—immediately adding the credibility that the team needed in 1998.

"It was incredibly important," Rose said. "To the 1998 and beyond Mets, it was as significant as what the Keith Hernandez acquisition meant to the Mets in 1983. I think we all remember what the Mets were until the Mets made the deal for Mike. We all pretty much used to call the Mets the same thing: 'a nice little team.' It was a team largely devoid of stars and made up of some good players and supported by players that no one other than Bobby Valentine believed in. When you add a guy like Mike Piazza, everything changes. The perception changed, and the Mets went from being 'a nice little team' and a relatively anonymous one to one that now had one of the biggest stars in the game. It created tremendous excitement for not only the short term, but beyond as well. But the caveat was that they were going to have to get him signed."

Therein lied the big question—could the Mets sign Piazza to a contract that would keep him in New York beyond the 1998 season? Early on in his tenure for the Blue and Orange, it didn't seem like a good fit. Piazza got off to a very rough start and was often booed and jeered at Shea Stadium. The questions about the contract every night also were taking their toll. Finally, Piazza decided to stop the contract talks altogether and just play ball.

"This is a crucial part of the year," Piazza told reporters. "I can't afford to go back and forth. The best situation would be to go the playoffs. That would make the decision easier. Right now, obviously, there is too much going on. I have to finish out my contract and play. A decision like that is not an overnight deal. There is a lot of soul-searching to be done. They have a lot to do too. I don't want it to drag out. It was the same with the Dodgers. I didn't want it to drag into the season."

Phillips backed up his new star, agreeing that it was time to focus on the game.

"This is mutually agreed upon," Phillips told reporters. "We talked about it, and I think from both sides' perspective, because there didn't seem to be a quick resolution to the negotiations, that we thought it would be better to get back to the focus on baseball. . . . We still hope and expect that at the end of the season we'll be able to sign him."

To close observers, such as Howie Rose, that decision to stop contract negotiations was critical to the long-term relationship between Piazza and the Mets.

"I thought that was the turning point in Mike's career with the Mets," Rose said. "He had the ability to be true to his word and put the contract talks on the back burner and just play baseball and let whatever contractually take care of itself. It couldn't have worked out any better. Mike separated himself from the business aspect and just went out and played, and he had a great stretch drive in '98, and when they had the window of exclusivity after the World Series that got him signed."

After the rough start, Mets fans finally embraced Piazza, who batted .348 in 109 games for the team, slamming 23 homers and driving in 76 runs. For the season, Piazza ended up with a combined 32 homers and 111 RBIs. Although the Mets did not reach the playoffs in 1998, all of the pieces now seemed to be in place, if they could sign the biggest piece to a long-term deal. On October 24, that is exactly what happened, when the Mets signed Piazza to the richest deal in Major League Baseball history—seven years for $91 million. Today, his number 31 is displayed proudly high atop Citi Field.

11

Fonzie Goes 6-for-6 (1999)

Few players in Mets history have been as beloved and—at the same time—as underrated as Edgardo "Fonzie" Alfonzo. In the late 1990s and early 2000s, Alfonzo was one of the best players in all of baseball. However, he was often overshadowed by members of his own team, including future Hall of Famer Mike Piazza and fellow infielder Robin Ventura. Despite the nickname, unlike the fictional tough guy from the television series *Happy Days*, Alfonzo kept a low profile.

It had been that way with Alfonzo since the Mets signed him as an undrafted free agent way back in 1991. From that time, the seventeen-year-old moved steadily up the Mets farm system and broke into the majors in 1995 at the age of twenty-one. He played second base, shortstop, and third base for the Mets early on but was moved to second base for good when the team acquired All-Star third baseman Robin Ventura following the 1998 season.

The move to second base did little to slow Alfonzo's offensive production, which continued to improve each year he was on the Mets. By 1999, Fonzie was ready to go from good to great. That season he batted .304 for the Mets, with 41 doubles, 27 home runs, and 108 runs batted in. He won the Silver Slugger Award, as the best-hitting second baseman in the National League, and finished eighth in the Most Valuable Player voting, just behind Piazza.

Throughout the summer, Alfonzo's defense at second base also was exemplary. In fact, the entire Mets infield was getting rave reviews. In the September issue of *Sports Illustrated*, the magazine cover featured a photo of Alfonzo, Ventura, first baseman John Olerud, and shortstop Rey Ordóñez. The headline on the cover asked "The Best Infield Ever?"

It was a great summer for the Mets, who were on their way to the playoffs for the first time since 1988. However, it was on August 30 of that year that Alfonzo etched himself into the Mets' record books forever.

In a matchup of playoff contenders, the second-place Mets entered the Astrodome to face the first-place Astros. The game was over before it started, with the Mets jumping out to a quick 7–0 lead after two innings. Alfonzo got the scoring parade going with a long, one-out home run in the top of the first inning. Thanks to the Mets' hot hitting on this night, Alfonzo would once again come to the plate in the top of the second inning, singling to right field and eventually scoring on a John Olerud double. This was just the start of Alfonzo's night, however.

In the top of the fourth inning, Alfonzo ripped into a pitch from Houston reliever Brian Williams for a two-run home run. By the end of four innings, Alfonzo was already 3-for-3 with 2 home runs and 3 runs scored. Two innings later, it became apparent that Alfonzo was having more than just your run-of-the-mill great night, when he crushed his 3rd home run of the game—his 4th hit and 4th run scored. Fonzie would clearly have at least one more at-bat in the game—and possibly more. In the top of the eighth inning, with the Mets leading 12–1, Alfonzo led off the inning with a line-drive single to left field. Later that inning he would score his 5th run of the game.

Thanks to the fact that the Mets were putting on an offensive display in Houston on this night, Alfonzo would get an incredible sixth at-bat in the nine-inning game.

"I was doing that game with Fran Healy in the Astrodome, and we were having a playful little discussion before Alfonzo came up for the last time, because at that point he had 3 home runs and was 5-for-5," said Mets broadcaster Howie Rose. "We were wondering what would be bigger: if he got the 4 home runs or it was just 6-for-6. I just remember how locked in he was that day. If any Met of that era was going to get 6 hits in a game, it was going to be Alfonzo."

Sure enough, Alfonzo got his opportunity in the top of the ninth inning and promptly ripped a double to right field. That completed a 6-for-6 night, with the

Edgardo Alfonzo watches the flight of his ninth-inning double—his sixth hit of the night against the Houston Astros.

supremely talented Alfonzo scoring 6 runs, a team record, along the way. This was how Rose described the call on Fox Sports New York:

> Line drive toward the right field corner—*fair ball*—Edgardo Alfonzo is 6-for-6. A ground-rule double that scores Todd Pratt. Edgardo Alfonzo is the first Met in team history with 6 hits in one game.

It was a historic night for Alfonzo, who, humble as always, took the whole thing in stride, saying after the game he was just happy that the Mets won.

"You talk about underrated players . . . Edgardo Alfonzo was underrated," Rose said. "He's as good a pure offensive player as [the Mets] have ever developed. You can put Cleon Jones, David Wright, and Edgardo Alfonzo on a very short list of tremendous offensive players that were ever developed by the Mets."

Alfonzo accomplished a few other milestones that night in Houston. He tied a Mets record with 3 home runs in a game, and his 16 total bases broke a record set by Darryl Strawberry in 1985. In addition, he became the first player to score 6 runs in a single game since Spike Owen did it in 1986 as a member of the Boston Red Sox.

However, as big as Alfonzo's outing was against the Astros on that August night, it is just one statistical example of how valuable Fonzie was during his career with the Mets, which was over far too quickly.

"He is, to this day, as classy a player as the Mets have ever had," Rose said. "He was a terrific hitter, he's a solid citizen, and, boy, you would love to have a couple of more Edgardo Alfonzos in your system."

12

The Rally (2000)

The Mets, in general, don't have a classic, natural rival, other than maybe the crosstown Yankees. Still, that's not a divisional rivalry—it's more of an emotional rivalry between the two fan bases. Having one consistent division rivalry, such as the Cardinals-Cubs or Yankees–Red Sox, has eluded the Mets. Instead, they have had different rivals depending on how good the other teams in the National League East are at any given time. Today, it's the Washington Nationals, in the 1980s it was the St. Louis Cardinals, etc. However, perhaps no rivalry was as heated for the Mets as the one between them and the Atlanta Braves in the 1990s into the early 2000s. At that time, the Braves were the class of the National League East, winning 14-straight division titles from 1991 through 2005, while the Mets went in and out of contention.

In 1999, the Mets would lose the National League Championship Series to the Braves, despite a certain Grand Slam Single. However, the heated rivalry only increased once the 1999 season came to a close, thanks to John Rocker, Atlanta's controversial closer. Known for riling up the Mets fans at Shea Stadium with his on-field antics, in December of 1999, he was the subject of a now infamous *Sports Illustrated* article in which he made many disparaging and controversial remarks about New York City, its inhabitants, and specifically Mets fans. Rocker immediately became public enemy number one in the Big Apple. So any time the Mets and Braves met during the 2000 season, there was some extra juice to an already intense rivalry.

Interestingly enough, Rocker was unavailable to pitch on the night of June 30, due to a callus on his hand. For most of the game, it didn't look like the Braves were going to need him. The first-place Braves were trying to hold off the Mets in the standings. One month earlier, the Braves had been 7½ games ahead of New York. Heading into the series, the Mets had cut that lead to just 2 games; however, the Braves took the opener to increase their lead to 3 games. It fully appeared that the lead would be extended to 4 games after the Friday-night affair, as the Braves had been dominating the game and leading 8–1 heading to the bottom of the eighth inning. Brian Jordan was leading the way for the Bravos, going 3-for-5 with a home run and 3 runs batted in. Pitcher Kevin Millwood, meanwhile, had shut the Mets down through seven strong innings, scattering 6 hits. Having thrown 112 pitches through the seven innings, Millwood did not come out for the eighth inning. He should have.

Instead, the Braves turned to seldom-used reliever Don Wengert to try to close out the Mets. Derek Bell of the Mets greeted Wengert with a single to center to lead off the inning. Innocent enough. Wengert then retired Edgardo Alfonzo on a deep fly to center. Mike Piazza then singled and advanced to second on an errant throw from the Atlanta shortstop, sending Bell to third base on the play. Robin Ventura then grounded out weakly to second base for the second out. Bell scored to make it 8–2, and Piazza crossed over to third base. There were now two outs with a man on third. Then, the madness started.

Todd Zeile stepped up and lined a single to center, scoring Piazza (8–3), followed by a Jay Payton single in front of Jordan in right field, moving Zeile to second base. Braves manager Bobby Cox had seen enough and replaced Wengert with Kerry Ligtenberg, who promptly walked the first batter he faced, Benny Agbayani, to load the bases. The next batter was pinch-hitter Mark Johnson, who just wanted to keep the rally going.

"I had been doing a lot of pinch-hitting for the Mets, and I knew that was going to be my role there," Johnson said. "Ideally, when you are pinch-hitting, you always want to be as aggressive as you can. You want to hit the first fastball that you see, but the Braves at that time were always pounding the outside corner, and that's what Kerry was trying to do. He was kind of nibbling on the outside corner, and I ended up walking. I was just happy to get on base and keep the rally going at that point."

Johnson's walk made the score 8–4, followed by yet another bases-loaded walk, this time to Melvin Mora, to make it 8–5. That was it for Ligtenberg, and

Cox turned to veteran Terry Mulholland to put the cork back in the bottle. He couldn't.

Bell, who had led off the inning with a single to center, drew another walk to force in a run (8–6). Braves pitchers had walked in three straight runs and Edgardo Alfonzo was the next batter. Mets broadcaster Gary Thorne on WPIX described the action:

> To third . . . base hit! No play at the plate—tie game! A two-RBI single for Edgardo Alfonzo!

The 52,831 fans at Shea, who had already been building up to a frenzy, exploded as the Mets tied the game, 8–8, and still had two runners on base. Two of those fans sitting in the stands were Mets broadcaster Howie Rose and his daughter. Because the game was on WPIX, Rose had the day off and was attending the game with his family. It's one of Rose's favorite moments he's had at the ballpark.

"For me, that one's very, very personal even though it's one that is also remembered by a lot of fans," Rose said. "I was not doing the game that night, and it was fireworks night, and I took my family to the game. We were sitting in the stands and I was sitting next to my older daughter, Alyssa, who was almost 11 at the time. Terry Mulholland, a left hander, is in the game, and the Mets had all of this momentum, and I just turned to Alyssa seconds before Mulholland threw the pitch and said, 'Piazza is going to hit a home run here.'"

Rose proved to be prophetic, as his colleague Gary Thorne described the action:

> Piazza rips it—will it stay faaaair? Goodbye! Home run! Mike Piazza a 3-run homer! 11–8!

"When he hit the home run, I'll never forget the look my daughter gave me, like, 'Oh my God, how did you know that?'" Rose remembered. "And she still brings that up to this day. So that's a very powerful moment for me, personally."

It was a powerful moment for Piazza and the Mets, as well. The Mets star pumped his fist after seeing the ball clear the wall, setting off an explosion of joy at Shea. In all, the Mets scored 10 runs on 6 hits and drew 4 walks in the bottom of the eighth inning.

"The thing I remember best about that inning is how good Fonzie and Mike were at that time," Johnson said. "The at-bats that they were having at that

Mike Piazza celebrates with teammates after blasting the rally-capping home run against the Atlanta Braves.

point in their careers, every at-bat was a great at-bat. We felt that if we could just get those guys back up in that spot, you had a good chance of coming back and scoring runs. Of course, at that time, Mike was just having an incredible season. Every time he seemed to get up in a big situation, he not only would get a big hit, he would hit a homer. The guy was unbelievable."

After the game, rather than take the attention on himself, Piazza put the victory in the full context of the pennant race.

"It's a big game for us," Piazza told reporters. "It's a great win for us. Fortunately for us, we snuck up on them. Hopefully, this is the type of win that gets you into the playoffs. Hopefully, this will relax us a little bit."

The Mets ended up splitting the four-game series with the Braves, who left town with the same 2-game lead in the division that they had when they arrived in New York.

"We showed Atlanta that we can play with them," Bell told reporters after the series. "We showed them that we can score runs off their pitchers. They know we're here and that we're not moving."

The Braves, in the end, finished 1 game ahead of the Mets and won the National League East once again. The Mets would have to settle for a Wild Card in 2000, but the two adversaries would never face off in the 2000 postseason. The Braves were swept away by the St. Louis Cardinals, and the Mets knocked off two teams not named the Atlanta Braves (Giants and Cardinals) to advance to the World Series. Still, when fans—and players—look back at certain moments of a season, the 10-run rally the Mets had against the Braves in 2000 will always be one of the moments that stands out.

It stood out enough for Piazza to mention it in his Hall of Fame speech in Cooperstown on July 24, 2016.

"As a matter of fact, one memorable 3-run home run that I hit in the 8th inning against the Braves," Piazza told the crowd of approximately 50,000 fans, "Edgardo [Alfonzo] actually had an amazing two-strike hit that tied the game and allowed me to relax and feel more confident at the plate knowing we were tied. A few guys up here know what that means."

For Mark Johnson, who played for the Mets for parts of three seasons and overall spent seven seasons in the majors, that night in late June of 2000 will always stand out as one of his best memories in the game.

"That game was definitely one of the best I played in," said Johnson, noting that he had several family members at the game because it was Fireworks Night at Shea. "I know we were down, but because it was Fireworks Night, people were sticking around, and the place was packed. I don't think I ever heard as much stomping and as much noise as I did as that rally unfolded. It was a big rivalry anyway, but to have that big comeback with a packed house, it was special."

13

"This One's Got a Chance!" (2001)

Author's Note: This is—in case you haven't noticed over the first 12 chapters—a baseball book, focusing almost completely on moments that took place on a baseball field. This chapter is no different than the others in that regard, other than the fact that I feel that it really needs to be put into the correct context. The moment that will be discussed—and celebrated—is Mike Piazza's mammoth home run against Steve Karsay of the Atlanta Braves on September 21, 2001. However, when put into the proper context—the fact that it was hit 10 days after the horrific attacks of September 11—the homer seems trivial. But the truth is, it helped to uplift a hurting city, if only for a moment.

"The September 21 home run transcends baseball," said Mets broadcaster Howie Rose. "It's one that I put on the back burner for a lot of years for a lot of reasons. I considered it so much more a piece of Americana and American history than Mets history and baseball history. I understand what it means much more now than I did then."

The night before the attacks, I watched from my couch as the Denver Broncos defeated the New York Giants on Monday Night Football. The game ended after midnight, it was a bad loss by the Giants, and I went to bed angry. However, by the next morning that game—or any other game, for that matter—meant nothing.

On the morning of Tuesday, September 11, the attacks occurred as I was on a Long Island Railroad train traveling from my home in Queens into Penn Station. While on the train, we learned what had happened. I remember clearly as I arrived at my midtown office my boss, and friend, Bill Falk—the editor-in-chief of the newsmagazine that I worked for and one of the biggest Mets fans I know—rightfully demanded that we not only continue working but also work even harder to get out our upcoming issue. We scrapped our original cover design, many of the inside pages, and got to work. Considering what was happening a few miles south of where we were, it was the very least we could do.

Sports had to stop mattering, at least for a little while. There were too many other things to care about, to worry about, to try to comprehend. Shea Stadium was no longer a baseball stadium—instead it was turned into a staging area for rescue efforts. The superstars in New York City were now the policemen, firefighters, and all of the first and second and third responders—the hundreds and hundreds of people who worked tirelessly at Ground Zero and all of the other sites around the nation where the attacks had taken place. Baseball didn't matter. Sports didn't matter. Real life had gotten in the way.

However, after Major League Baseball suspended play for nearly a week, the Mets resumed their season in Pittsburgh on September 17 and went on to sweep a three-game series against the Pirates. The question was, what would it be like to have a major event in New York City? Were we ready?

As the days rolled on and New Yorkers tried to get back to some semblance of a "normal" routine, it was time to consider resuming our usual activities. Mike Vaccaro of the *New York Post* explained it best: "Exactly 10 days after the city had its heart broken and its soul turned inside-out, the first professional sporting event in New York's new normal would take place: Mets-Braves, 7:10 p.m., Friday night, Shea Stadium."

★ ★ ★

"There were a bunch of us who didn't even want to be there because it was such a sorrowful time in our nation's history," Rose said. "Believe me, I drove to the ballpark with a lot of trepidation knowing it was going to be the first time since September 11 that you were going to have 50 thousand people gathered in one spot. That was very intimidating."

Prior to the start of the game between the Mets and Braves, the two teams exchanged handshakes and hugs on the field, with all of the players wearing baseball caps representing the NYPD, NYFD, Port Authority Police, and other service and rescue agencies. It was a unique start to a unique night.

Once back between the lines, the game seemed to be just that—a baseball game. Although it was far from just a baseball game—all you had to do was look at the players' faces or glance into the crowd to know that. From the first pitch, the game was a bit lackluster, as the Mets and Braves each scored 1 run in the fourth inning—the Braves on a Ken Caminiti double and the Mets on a Tsuyoshi Shinjo sacrifice fly. In the top of the eighth inning, an exhausted crowd watched helplessly as the Braves' Brian Jordan stroked a run-scoring double in the top of the eighth inning to give Atlanta a 2–1 lead.

In the bottom of the eighth inning, Matt Lawton led off for the Mets with a groundball to shortstop for the first out. Edgardo Alfonzo then walked. The next batter was Mike Piazza, who was already 2-for-3 with 2 doubles. The

The Mets and Braves, rivals on the field, shared a special moment before the start of the game.

first pitch from Karsay was a called strike. The next pitch was down and on the outside portion of the plate, and Piazza was able to extend his arms, allowing him to do what he did best. Howie Rose of FSN New York provided the words:

It's hit deep to left-center, Andruw Jones on the run, this one's got a chance—home run!—Mike Piazza!—and the Mets lead 3–2!

"To me it wasn't really a call, it was just knowing how much or how little to say," Rose said. "The funny thing about that call is that a former Mets employee would always tease me when they played it because off the bat I said, 'This one's got a chance.' He would always say to me, 'Hey, you think that ball had a chance? That ball went about 440 feet!'"

True enough, Piazza's home run was absolutely crushed, flying high over the left-center field cameramen who stood on top of a scaffolding. However, "this one's got a chance" has lived on, while the home run itself has become something of legend. Still, Rose understands why his call has become such a big part of the moment.

"I think probably people relate more to the fact that Piazza hit this home run and maybe my voice, as a guy who had already been around for a little while, might have provided some comfort or connection that in a sense is a familial connection because you are part of fans' daily lives for six or seven months," Rose said.

One of the things Rose remembers best is how his broadcasting partner—former major leaguer Fran Healy—reacted to the home run.

"The funny thing about that game was that we were under orders from the executives from MSG to not emote because it was a very solemn occasion," Rose recalled. "They said 'whatever you do, do not make any reference or mentions of bombs, explosions, or anything that would conjure up images

An emotional Mike Piazza salutes the fans after hitting one of the biggest home runs in Mets' history.

that people were still trying to push aside.' So I was working with Fran Healy that night, and Fran hated taking direction. He was going to do what he was going to do. If you listen to the tape, after Piazza gets back into the dugout, this was Fran's moment of defiance. Healy said, 'This place was just waiting to *explode* . . . This place just *ex-ploded,*' and he kept on hitting hard and emphasizing the word *exploded*, and that was his way of showing management what he thought of their edict."

As the years have gone on, Piazza's home run has only become more and more legendary. During his Hall of Fame induction speech to approximately 50 thousand fans assembled in Cooperstown during the summer of 2016, Piazza spoke openly about how the entire situation affected him.

"Many of you give me praise for the 2-run home run on the first game back on September 21 to push us ahead of the rival Braves," Piazza said. "But true praise belongs to police, firefighters, first responders, who knew that they were going to die but went forward anyway."

Piazza's Hall of Fame plaque really says it all. It reads, in part—"Led the Mets to the 2000 Subway Series, and helped rally a nation one year later with his home run in the first Mets game in New York following the 9/11 attacks."

14

Yes! A No-No! (2012)

Benjamin Franklin is known for a lot of things. After all, he is one of the founding fathers of our country. He was a scientist, a politician, an inventor, a statesman, and a pretty amazing person. He also said, and wrote, some pretty amazing things. One of his most famous lines was written in a letter to French physicist Jean-Baptiste LeRoy in 1789. It said, in part, "In this world nothing can be said to be certain, except death and taxes." However, there was a later draft of that letter that is lesser known. It read, in part, "In this world nothing can be said to be certain, except death, taxes, and the fact that no member of the Mets will ever pitch a no-hitter." Franklin, who was a big fan of his hometown Philadelphia Phillies, clearly sensed the divisional rivalry to come. Forget the fact that the Phillies were not founded until nearly one hundred years after Franklin's death. Remember, Ben Franklin was known as a man who was always ahead of his time, and a Phillies fan would never wish anything good on the Mets.

Mets fans, on the other hand—as they had for the past 8,019 games—were hoping to see something special when Johan Santana took the mound at Citi Field, 222 years after Franklin's death.

"There are days that I still can't believe that it happened and wonder it if will ever happen again," said Mets broadcaster Howie Rose.

Rose, not unlike most—if not all—Mets fans, was sure that *it* would never happen. The Mets, after all, have always been blessed with top pitching talent. They have also seemed to have a curse hanging over them. Through the 2011 season, Mets pitchers had thrown 35 one-hitters—but never a no-hitter. The most famous of the close calls, of course, was Tom Seaver's near perfect game in July of 1969 against the Chicago Cubs (see chapter 2). Seaver had four other one-hitters for the Mets, the most painful of which was on July 4, 1972, when he lost his bid for a no-hitter on a broken-bat liner with one out in the ninth inning. That afternoon, it was reserve Leron Lee who played the role of Jimmy Qualls.

"When the whole thing was over, I was more disappointed, I think, about the pitch that Lee hit," Seaver told reporters after the game. "But I knew it was a good pitch. . . . You have to win the game. That's what counts."

For whatever reason, for 50 years the Mets could not record a no-hitter. Ben Franklin, seemingly, was correct. Then, on February 2, 2008, the Mets made a blockbuster trade, acquiring Minnesota Twins pitching ace Johan Santana in exchange for four players. After making the trade, the Mets signed the southpaw to a six-year, $137.5 million contract.

Santana's resume was outstanding. Over the past four seasons with the Twins, he had won two Cy Young Awards as the top pitcher in the American League, where he averaged 18 wins and 246 strikeouts per season. His first season with the Mets was Santana-esqe, as he won 16 games, struck out 206 batters, and led the league with a 2.53 earned-run average.

Unfortunately for Santana and the Mets, 2009 and 2010 did not go as smoothly, as the Mets' ace suffered through various injuries. Still, following the 2009 season he was named number 3 on the list of the 50 greatest current players in baseball by the *Sporting News*. However, the injuries piled up, and Santana was forced to miss the entire 2011 season while he recovered from his shoulder surgery.

Heading into the 2012 season, no one was quite sure what Santana was going to be able to give the Mets. The last thing on anyone's mind was that he would be making history. Early in spring training, Santana joked with reporters who were impressed at how well he looked on the mound.

"You're making this a big deal," he said, smiling, to a group of reporters. "It's like I've never thrown a baseball before."

By the end of spring training, Santana was excited, knowing he was healthy enough to be penciled in as the Opening Day starter.

"It's great, man, it's great," Santana told reporters. "I worked hard, and to be here right now and to be able to do everything the way it was supposed to be done is huge for me."

Santana went on to start the opener for the Mets, the first time he stood on a major-league mound since September of 2010. He pitched five scoreless innings—victory unto itself. In his first 10 starts of 2012, Santana went 2–2 with an ERA of 2.75. His 10th start was his best, throwing a shutout against the San Diego Padres. He only needed 96 pitches to get through the nine innings. Heading into his 11th start of the season, all eyes were on Santana to see how his surgically repaired shoulder would react to him having pitched nine innings.

Pitcher Johan Santana after doing the impossible—pitching a no-hitter for the Mets.

"There's so much about that night," Rose said. "Santana was coming off of pitching a complete game his last time out and of course was not so far removed from very serious shoulder surgery. There was a lot of concern about his pitch count and all of the questions to Terry [Collins] before the game were how long he was going to let Santana go. Terry told us, '110 to 115 tops,' and we took that as gospel."

By 2012, the Mets not having a no-hitter had already become one of the most well-known facts in baseball. Of the 30 teams in the majors, only the Mets and San Diego Padres had never had a pitcher complete the feat. Santana's 11th start was on June 1 against the St. Louis Cardinals in front of 27,069 fans at Citi Field. Although Santana got off to a good start, he was throwing a lot of pitches early in the game. Seemingly, there would be no history made that night.

"Santana walked a bunch of people early in the game, and I actually said on the air after the Cardinals went through about five innings without a hit, 'Well, if you think tonight is going to be the night, forget it because he's on a very strict pitch limit,'" Rose remembered. "That was the backdrop of the last few innings, not whether he would pitch a no-hitter, but would he be around to attempt the no-hitter."

As the game moved along, Santana received a little help on the way to making history. The first moment came in the top of the sixth inning, when Carlos Beltrán grounded out weakly to third base to lead off the inning. However, what the box score doesn't tell you—but instant replay does—is that Beltrán actually might have gotten a base hit earlier in the at-bat. But he didn't. In 2012 there was no instant replay used in the game, and third-base umpire Adrian Johnson threw both of his arms up emphatically to say that the ball was foul. The St. Louis third-base coach chirped, and Beltrán gave a prolonged stare down the third-base line, but none of it mattered. Foul ball.

One inning later, Santana's left fielder made his mark when Mike Baxter made a circus catch off of Yadier Molina's long drive, slamming into the wall and breaking his collarbone on the play.

There always seemed to be an incredible catch in a no-hitter, and therefore the no-hit dream appeared closer after that play. However, cause for concern was the fact that Santana's pitch count continued to rise.

"You can see Terry was dying in the dugout," Rose said. "This was eating him up. However this ends up, Terry is now going to be a tormented man."

Finally, the ninth inning had arrived, and Santana had three more outs to get. Other men had been here before. None had accomplished what they had set out to do.

The first batter was Matt Holliday.

"Holliday hit a sinking liner off the end of the bat, and I thought, *that's dropping* because I could see the ball was going to drop, and Andres Torres closed real fast on it and made the catch," Rose said.

One out.

The next batter was Allen Craig, who hit the ball well, but right to the left fielder. Kirk Nieuwenhuis, who had moved from center to left to replace the injured Baxter, was right there and made the catch.

Two outs.

Santana was now just one out away from immortality.

The next batter was David Freese. However, from the Mets radio booth, Rose was more concerned with the man on deck for the Cardinals.

"So here it is, David Freese against Johan Santana, and of all the people in the world to be waiting on deck if Freese got on with a walk was Yadier Molina," Rose said. "I knew for a fact if he walked Freese, Molina was going to hit a home run. That we knew."

Santana, his pitch count now at 128, started by throwing three straight balls to Freese—a 3–0 count, and Molina lurked. Santana fought back to make it 3 balls and 2 strikes.

Then, it happened.

"He throws him a great change, Freese swings and misses and even though I'm talking, I don't even know what I'm saying because I'm in complete shock," Rose said.

Here's how it sounded from Rose on WFAN radio:

Santana into the windup . . . the payoff pitch on the way . . . swung on and missed strike three . . . he's done it . . . Johan Santana has pitched a no-hitter in the 8,020th game in the history of the New York Mets. They finally have a no-hitter, and who better to do it than Johan Santana, and what a remarkable story. . . . His teammates are mobbing him at the mound.

"I did not believe that he had pitched a no-hitter until probably a second after the ball was in [catcher] Josh Thole's glove because I had trained myself to, however begrudgingly, accept the fact that no Met was ever going to pitch a no-hitter," Rose said. "For whatever reason, it just seemed the baseball fates had determined that this franchise—even with a lot of really terrific pitchers over the years—was never going to have a no-hitter."

That all ended on June 1, 2012.

One of the men who could most appreciate what Santana had done was Tom Seaver, who spoke to Richard Sandomir of the *New York Times* the following day.

"I'm not surprised that he did it," said Seaver, who pitched the only no-hitter of his own career in 1978 as a member of the Cincinnati Reds—also against the Cardinals. "He's a hell of a pitcher. It's really nice that a pitcher of his caliber level did it. It adds a shine to it that it's a pitcher of his credibility. . . . To me, it's nice that it's off the table now. It's great for the franchise that they have it now because it was always a topic of conversation."

Another New York sports writer, Stefan Bondy of the New York *Daily News*, got the reaction from another man who is well known to Mets fans.

"I don't know, I was kind of rooting for him," Jimmy Qualls said. "They kept bringing it up, how there hadn't been one for the history of the Mets. I was just kind of rooting for him."

The win may have proved costly for Santana, who was never quite the same after that magical night. The 134 pitches seemed to take their toll on the lefty. He would appear in 10 more games that season, posting an earned-run average of more than 8.00. Following the end of the 2012 season, Santana would not throw another pitch in the majors.

In 2013, Santana once again needed surgery on his throwing shoulder and, despite numerous attempts at a comeback, was never able to make it back to the big leagues.

However, Santana in no way blames the game on June 1 for ending his career. On the contrary, in an interview with *Sports Illustrated* in 2015, he explained how important it was for him to finish that game. "Even if an army had come to get me, I wouldn't have come out of the game," he told the magazine.

15

DeGrom Is a Star (2015)

In 2015, it was Jacob deGrom's turn to shine on the big stage—and that is exactly what he did. To understand the true spirit of his all-star performance, however, you need to go all the way back to 1967. Prior to that, the Mets' representative in the All-Star Game was merely there because every team had to have a representative. From 1962 through 1966, players such as Richie Ashburn, Duke Snider, Ed Kranepool, and Ron Hunt served as the Mets' honoree in the midsummer classic. In 1967, however, things changed. That year, the Mets had a rookie pitcher by the name of Tom Seaver, who had 8 wins at the break. Seaver came on in the bottom of the 15th inning at Anaheim Stadium to record the final three outs and secure the victory for the National League. It also, however, secured something else—respectability for a franchise that had been seen as something of a joke in years past.

"I just remember how cool it was in '67," said Mets broadcaster Howie Rose. "It was exciting to think that the Mets had made a footprint in the All-Star Game, even though they would still go on to lose 100 games that year."

Mets pitchers would continue to make an impact in the All-Star Game over the years, as Jon Matlack was named co-MVP in the 1975 midsummer classic, and Doc Gooden would turn heads in the 1984 game.

In 2013, with the Mets playing host to the All-Star Game for the first time since 1964, Matt Harvey was named the starting pitcher for the National League—to the delight of all Mets fans. After a shaky beginning to his start—

including a leadoff double by Mike Trout and the drilling of the Yankees' Robinson Canó in the knee with a fastball—Harvey responded by striking out Miguel Cabrera, forcing Chris Davis to fly out, and finishing the inning by striking out José Bautista. He then retired the American League 1-2-3 in the top of the second inning and left the mound to an explosion of applause. It was a moment to remember for the hometown ace.

"Oh, it was absolutely so much fun," Harvey told reporters after the game. "Just being in the locker room with all the guys, the whole experience, the red carpet, it being in New York, and starting. As a kid I don't think you could have dreamed of doing something like that. It was a tremendous honor and something I am very thankful for."

Two years later, in the top of the sixth inning in Cincinnati, it was deGrom's turn to star on the big stage—and he decided to up the ante. The American League quickly learned why deGrom was named the 2014 National League Rookie of the Year.

The first batter to face deGrom was Stephen Vogt of the Oakland Athletics—fastball on the outside corner for a strike, fastball down the middle for strike two, fastball up, swinging strike three—one out. The next batter was Jason Kipnis of the Cleveland Indians—fastball on the inside corner for a strike, fastball that split the plate for strike two, ball one a little outside, swinging strike three—two outs. The third batter to face deGrom was José Iglesias of the Detroit Tigers—strike one swinging, strike two swinging on a pitch in the dirt, swinging strike three, again on a pitch in the dirt—three outs, inning over. The asterisk is there to remind you that it is the only pitch that deGrom threw in the inning that was not a strike. The Mets second-year pitcher had just come on to the biggest stage in baseball and struck out three American League All-Stars on 10 pitches.

"That was unreal," deGrom told reporters after the game. "I was looking forward to getting a chance to throw, and I was pretty nervous in the bullpen, but when I got out there, the nerves kind of went away. And it was an awesome experience."

Following the game, Kipnis remembered it a little differently.

"It was good morning, good afternoon, ball outside, goodnight," Kipnis said, describing his four-pitch at-bat to reporters following the game. "He's a power pitcher, a strong pitcher and a damn good one, and I got to see it tonight."

It was the latest in a long line of Mets success in all-star games. In addition to all of the pitching performances, there were the heroics by Lee Mazzilli in 1979,

Jacob deGrom delivers a pitch during the 2015 All-Star Game.

the time the Mets had five All-Star representatives in 1986, and David Wright's All-Star home run in 2006. None of those performances, however, surpass what deGrom did on that night in Cincinnati, establishing that he was going to be a force to be reckoned with for years to come.

Perhaps the greatest quote that came after deGrom's performance came from the man who led off the inning against him—Stephen Vogt. When reporters gathered after the game to speak to Vogt and asked him what it was like to get a chance to bat in the All-Star Game, the thirty-year-old responded: "I got a chance to strike out. [DeGrom] was some kind of good."

16

The Trade That Never Was (2015)

On July 29, 2015, the Mets traded one of their top young pitchers, Zack Wheeler, along with infielder Wilmer Flores, to the Milwaukee Brewers for outfielder Carlos Gomez. However, don't try to find any statistics from Wheeler or Flores on the Brewers website—and, for that matter, you won't see any stories about Gomez in the Mets' archive.

As the trading deadline quickly approached, the Mets were rumored to be involved in various trade talks. The team had been playing uninspired baseball all season and was in major need of a boost. Names like Jay Bruce, Yoenis Céspedes, and others had been thrown around for weeks. However, it was Gomez that the Mets decided would be their man.

"It's a done deal #Mets are getting Gomez," tweeted Joel Sherman of the *New York Post* at 8:57 p.m. A few minutes later, Andy Martino of the New York *Daily News* tweeted the exact same thing. A few minutes later, Sherman tweeted again that the deal was "pending physicals"—a mere formality in the world of sports trades. Reportedly, Gomez was told about the deal.

By 9:46 p.m., news of the trade had made its way through the stands at Citi Field, where the Mets were playing the San Diego Padres. It was quite surreal actually; the fans knew Flores had been traded before he knew. During one of his at-bats, they gave him a standing ovation to say thank you—and goodbye. When he went back out to second base—yes, the Mets kept him in the game—he was clearly upset and wiped tears away from his face. Flores had been a part of the

Mets organization since he was a young teenager. The thought of being traded—and finding out the way he was finding out—seemed implausible.

Then, at 9:54 p.m.—some doubt. Ken Rosenthal of FOX Sports tweeted, "Asked official involved with Gomez trade why Flores is still in game. Reply: 'No deal is done. The entire world has jumped the gun.'"

Following the game, Mets manager Terry Collins was clearly angry—not knowing anything about the potential trade.

"Someone came to me and said, 'Wilmer's crying,'" Collins told reporters, recounting a conversation that had taken place in the dugout during the game. "I said, 'Why?' 'Well, he got traded.' 'To who? For what?'"

Finally, at 10:53 p.m., Jared Diamond of the *Wall Street Journal* tweeted, "Sandy Alderson says that the trade for Carlos Gomez 'will not transpire.'"

"Unfortunately, social media, etc., got ahead of the facts, and it may have had an adverse effect on one of the players rumored to be involved," Alderson told reporters about the circumstances and how Flores reacted. "It's one of those things that happens today with modern communications, etc. It's an unfortunate situation, but whatever has been speculated over the course of the evening has not and will not transpire."

An hour and a half later, Rosenthal tweeted, "Sources: #Mets backed out of trade due to concern over hip issue with #Brewers' Gomez."

The deal was dead.

The next day it appeared as though the Mets had found their man—again. It was going to be Cincinnati Reds outfielder Jay Bruce to the rescue in Flushing—and the blogs were buzzing: "The Mets and Reds worked through the night on a Jay Bruce trade, and this morning the deal appears close to fruition. ESPN New York is reporting that the two teams are reviewing medical information and are nearing the completion of a trade that would send Zack Wheeler to Cincinnati and Bruce to New York," read a post on SB Nation's *Amazin' Avenue*. However, the Bruce trade—like the Gomez trade—was not to be.

Instead—two days after the nontrade—the Mets pulled off a blockbuster by sending prospects Michael Fulmer and Luis Cessa to the Detroit Tigers for slugger Yoenis Céspedes.

"We believe we're in position to compete through the rest of the season for a playoff spot," Alderson told reporters, "and we're going to do everything we can to ensure that competitive level. . . . This is the kind of player that can have a big impact both in terms of the game on the field and how the team is perceived."

The 2015 trading deadline was an extremely emotional one for Wilmer Flores.

The Mets had made their big trade, and Flores, it turned out, was staying put. He celebrated in style the night the Mets got Céspedes by slugging a game-winning walk-off home run against the Washington Nationals. From tears to jubilation, he proved that Jimmy Dugan was wrong, and there certainly is crying in baseball. The Flores homer—and the arrival of Céspedes—sparked a sinking Mets team to win seven straight games and 11 of their next 13. More importantly, it galvanized the team, which would ride the wave that crested at the trading deadline all the way to the World Series.

17

Colón Goes Deep (2016)

On September 18, 2000, Bartolo Colón—in his fourth season with the Cleveland Indians—took the mound at Yankee Stadium and completely baffled the defending world champions. This was not a second-rate lineup that Colón was facing—it was Derek Jeter, David Justice, Tino Martinez, Jorge Posada, etc. However, Colón made the Yankees—who were en route to their third straight title and fourth in five years—look like Little Leaguers. He allowed no hits until the bottom of the eighth inning when Luis Polonia singled up the middle for the only hit of the game, struck out 13, and walked only 1. Author's note: It was one of the most exciting games I have ever witnessed in person. To have been in Yankee Stadium to watch a no-hitter against the Yankees—well, that would have been priceless.

Between that day and the day he became a member of the Mets, Colón won more than 130 ball games.

Colón—who arrived in Flushing in 2014—immediately became a fan favorite. The larger-than-life, seemingly happy-go-lucky pitcher came to be known to Mets fans, affectionately, as "Big Sexy." That first season, Colón surpassed all expectations by winning 15 games for the Mets, followed with a 14-win season in 2015, and another 15-win season in 2016. Colón had quickly become known—on a team of young superstar pitchers—as one of the most reliable pitchers on the staff. He could start, he could pitch in relief, and he was probably the only pitcher alive with no innings limit.

Colón had plenty of experience to draw from by the time he arrived on the Mets. He spent the first five-and-a-half years of his career with the Cleveland Indians but was traded to the Montreal Expos in the summer of 2002. The back of Colón's baseball card would become legendary from there—in 2003 he played for the Chicago White Sox; from 2004 to 2007 he played for the Anaheim/Los Angeles Angels; in 2008 he played for the Boston Red Sox; in 2009 he returned to the White Sox; in 2011—after missing the entire 2010 season with an injury— he played for the Yankees; from 2012 to 2013 he played for the Oakland Athletics. Whew! If you add that he had played for two additional teams since leaving the Mets following the 2016 season, through the 2017 season Colón has played in the majors for 20 years and 10 teams. By 2017, he completed the impressive feat of defeating every single one of the 30 major league teams.

Colón was not just another pitcher, however, as he was named an All-Star four times and won the American League Cy Young Award in 2005. He has won 15 or more games during a single season nine times and has pitched more than 200 innings in a season eight times. Despite all of these accomplishments, however, there is one thing he does not do well—hit. Not that he had too many opportunities throughout most of his career. Before coming to the Mets, he had started only 17 games for a National League team. Otherwise, he was relegated to interleague play at-bats. In all, before arriving to the Mets Colón had 96 career at-bats, reaching base safely 10 times—a batting average of .104.

In Colón's first season with the Mets, he managed to scratch out 2 hits—a single and a double. Colón's at-bats quickly had become one of the most anticipated events of his starts, as the big man would always swing with everything he had, often causing his helmet to fly off. The fans at Citi Field appreciated the effort. In 2015, that effort paid off as Colón stroked 8 hits, including one double and 4 runs batted in. Heading into the 2016 season, there was very little in the game that Colón had not accomplished. He had not, however, legged out a triple—and let's face it, that wasn't going to happen. Only one thing might have been less likely—a Bartolo Colón home run.

"We always used to joke around and have fun with it because everyone loved his at-bats, but I think something that gets lost is how hard Bartolo had worked to not be an embarrassment at the plate," said SNY on-field reporter Steve Gelbs. "He didn't want to be an automatic out, but of course nobody expected he would hit a home run—ever."

On Saturday, May 7, 2016, Colón and the Mets were facing the San Diego Padres in the third game of a four-game series at Petco Park. There was nothing unusual about this game at first glance—well, except for the fact that more than 1,400 7-Line Army fans were in attendance that day. The 7-Line, as it always does at home and on the road, made their presence known, and in the top of the second inning they were a part of a Mets miracle moment. With two outs and nobody on, catcher Kevin Plawecki doubled to deep center field. At the time, the Mets were probably satisfied that Colón would get the chance to hit in the inning so that the leadoff hitter could bat first in the third inning. Gelbs, who was in his first full season covering the Mets on a daily basis, decided he would take the opportunity to move from one location to another. He was surely not going to miss much, as Colón stepped in. However, the pitcher—who had not yet had a hit in 2016—had other ideas, as Gary Cohen told the world on WPIX-TV:

> Colón looking for his first hit of the season—*and he drives one, deep to left field. Back goes Upton, back near the wall—it's outta here!*

Cohen's excitement matched that of every Mets fan who was listening to him:

> *Bartolo has done it! The impossible has happened!* His first career home run!

"So here is one of the great career regrets that I have ever had," Gelbs said with a hearty laugh. "I was walking to a different position in the stadium and did not witness the home run. I was walking and heard Gary Cohen go crazy in my earpiece and by the time I jetted out to see what was going on it was already too late. That's about as excited as I've ever heard Gary, and I think that was one of the greatest calls ever.

After the game, Colón was—as usual—smiling.

"It means a lot," Colón told reporters through an interpreter after the game. "It's something that I still can't believe until now."

Hitting the home run, it turns out, was only the beginning. After carrying his bat with him all the way to first base, Colón went on a majestic—and lengthy—trot around the bases. When he finally touched home plate and returned to the dugout, only the on-deck hitter and manager Terry Collins were there to shake his hand.

Pitcher Bartolo Colón is greeted at home plate after smashing his miraculous homer.

Howie Rose, the voice of the Mets on 710 WOR Radio, described it best:

They are going to give him the silent treatment in the dugout; they have vacated—the Mets have left the building. Bartolo Colón is the loneliest man in San Diego . . . after hitting a home run, and there's nobody there to greet him. And now, here they come up the dugout steps—wow!

"I did see him slowly rounding the bases and then going into the dugout and being greeted by absolutely nobody," Gelbs said.

Having so many Mets fans at the game only enhanced the experience. And to cap things off, a Mets fan who was originally from New Jersey caught the ball—and returned it to Colón.

"What I remember about the rest of the day and the day after was that the 7-Line Army being in San Diego changed the whole tenor of the day," Gelbs said. "To have such a strong fan base there making a ton of noise, it almost felt like it happened—not necessarily at home—but as close as you can get to it on the road. It was a moment that you never thought would ever take place, and then it also happened on a day where there just happened to be a couple of thousand Mets fans that made the trek out there. A Met fan caught the baseball, and it was a really cool moment for sure."

PART TWO

POSTSEASON MOMENTS

There has long been debate over the origin of the proverb "Absence makes the heart grow fonder." Although it could date back as far as the 1600s, it is equally possible that it was uttered by a fan of the Blue and Orange—referring to the team's fleeting number of postseason appearances. No matter who originally said it, all Mets fans can certainly relate to it.

Of the nine times the Mets have reached the postseason, they have made the most of their opportunities. New York has won five National League pennants and two World Series titles. In each of those nine trips to the playoffs, there has been no shortage of memorable moments.

Of course, the Mets' first postseason run is arguably the most well known— and seemingly the most miraculous. No one, including the Mets themselves, thought they would be able win the National League's Eastern Division, let alone beat the 100:1 odds and win the World Series. Finishing a distant second place seemed to be the ultimate possibility in 1969. "The supreme optimist says we'll finish second in the Eastern Division of the league," Tom Seaver told reporters in March of 1969. "The only team we can't catch is St. Louis. The only other team we may have to fight off is Chicago. But we can beat Pittsburgh, Philadelphia, and Montreal. Who's the supreme optimist? Me."

Even after winning 100 games during the regular season and sweeping the Atlanta Braves in the very first NLCS, the Mets were having a hard time getting any respect from the American League champion and heavily favored Baltimore Orioles. "We still don't know if they're for real," Baltimore slugger Boog Powell told reporters before the start of the World Series. Outfielder Paul Blair added, "Two pitchers, some slap hitters, and a little speed. . . . we have a better ball club, and if we play our ball game, the emotions of the fans and all of this talk isn't going to help them at all." Spoiler alert—the Mets were for real.

There are 14 moments in Part II of this book, highlighting memories from seven of the Mets' nine postseason runs. Whether it was Seaver, Koosman, Clendenon, and the Amazin' Mets of 1969; Matlack, Harrelson, McGraw, and the never-say-die team of 1973; Carter, Strawberry, Hernandez, and the powerhouse 1986 squad; or the other great postseason runs, there are memories aplenty for all fans. From Paul Lo Duca tagging out two runners on one play, to Endy Chavez jumping out of his shoes to make the catch, or Todd Pratt—yes, Todd Pratt— hitting his incredible home run, the Mets' playoff runs had it all. All you need to do is sit back, turn the page, and relive the excitement!

18

The Amazin' Mets (1969)

Spoiler alert for this chapter—do not continue to read if you do not want to find out how the 1969 baseball season ended. OK, here it is—but you were warned—the New York Mets won the 1969 World Series! And yes, it was amazin'!

At the end of the 1969 season, the New York Mets shocked the baseball world when they accomplished what fans across the country thought otherwise impossible. NBC Radio announcer Bill O'Donnell described the final out of baseball's most improbable outcome at 3:14 p.m. on October 16, 1969:

> Fly ball, deep left field, Jones is back to the fence—the World Series is over, Jones makes the catch.

Of all of the amazing things that happened during the summer of '69, the Mets becoming champions was the unlikeliest of them all. In fact, Vegas oddsmakers had the Mets at 100:1 to win the National League pennant before the season began. There was a better chance that man would walk on the moon, it seemed—which happened that summer too and was considered a marvel of its time. Still, the Mets going on to win the World Series nearly three months later seemed like an even longer shot. It would have to be one giant step for 25 men.

Around the time that Neil Armstrong and Buzz Aldrin were hanging out on the moon, the Mets were just floating in the atmosphere of the National League

East. The Mets, who had finished ninth in the National League in 1968, moved into second place on June 3, 1969—8½ games behind the Chicago Cubs.

Later that summer, after the Mets defeated the Montreal Expos 5–2, they came within 3 games of the Cubs. However, the team then fell into a tailspin, and over the next month plummeted to 10 games behind Chicago, causing fans to limit their expectations. But the 1969 Mets were not your usual team. They had a flair for the unlikely.

Beginning on August 16, the Mets won 12 of their next 13 games, while the Cubs played sub .500 ball during that same span, helping close the gap for the Mets, then just 2½ games out of first place. As the summer ended and the calendar flipped to September, the Mets really started to make their move, led by their two aces at the top of the rotation.

Beginning on September 5, with the Mets trailing the Cubs by 5 games in the standings, Tom Seaver and Jerry Koosman combined to go 11–0. Dating back a little earlier, Seaver and Koosman combined to win 18 of their final 19 decisions in 1969.

"That happened when that breath of cool air started hitting New York after the dog days of summer," said Koosman, who went 17–9 with an earned run average of 2.28 in 1969 and—along with Seaver—provided the best one-two punch by starting pitchers in the National League. "A lot of us pitchers didn't like that heat. But once that cool air started to blow in, you get your second wind, so to speak, and we got hot."

On Septembe 9, with the Mets trailing the Cubs by just 1½ games, divine intervention stepped in—on four legs, no less. In the top of the fourth inning, the game was briefly interrupted when a black cat appeared out of nowhere, paused in the Cubs' on-deck circle, and ran past the Cubs dugout on its way under the stands at Shea. The Mets went on to win the game 7–1 behind Seaver and pulled within a half game of first place. Whether it was due to the forces of the black cat, great pitching, timely hitting, or all of the above, there was no stopping the Mets, who won their next six games to move comfortably into first place. For the month of September the Mets went 23–7, and on September 24, they completed the first step of their impossible dream.

"We knew we were going to clinch it because we had gotten so far in front. It was just a matter of when," said Koosman, noting that by the time the Mets clinched the National League East they had moved 6 games ahead of the reeling Cubs, who closed out the final month with a record of 8–17. "I remember [Gary]

Gentry pitching, and we really just wanted to get it over and done with and were ready to move on."

Gentry provided exactly what Koosman and his teammates were hoping for, scattering 4 hits against the St. Louis Cardinals en route to a 6–0 victory. The final out came when Gentry induced, of all people, Joe Torre to ground into a game-ending double play. Broadcaster Lindsey Nelson provided the words:

> Groundball to short, this could be it—there's one, there's two—the game is over, and the Mets are the champions! At 9:07 on September 24th, the Mets have won the championship of the Eastern Division of the National League.

Mets fans went berserk, storming the field and literally ripping it to shreds. Fans stole home plate, the pitching rubber, and two of the three bases. One fan tried to scale the giant scoreboard in right field, only to fall from 25 feet, breaking both of his legs—a small price to pay, apparently, to advance to the postseason.

"We'll have the field back in shape in a couple of days," Mets Vice President James K. Thomson told reporters. "It looks worse than it is. We had 300 policemen and 332 ushers on duty, but what could they do? [The fans] were all in good spirits. They just wanted to take home some souvenirs from this historic event."

As the Mets celebrated in their clubhouse, Mets manager Gil Hodges took some time to enjoy the moment.

"They're a great bunch of boys," he told reporters in the clubhouse. "They showed confidence, maturity, togetherness—and pitching. They proved it could be done. Oh yes, I'm excited, thrilled, very happy—not quite as much as when I was a player, maybe, but all of those things."

The Mets had only about a week before the playoffs would start but continued to play hard night in and night out, finishing the season winning nine of their final 10 games and 100 victories total. It was the first winning season in team history. But there was more to come. For the first time in history, there would be something called a National League Championship Series where the Mets would have to face the champions of the National League West, the Atlanta Braves. The Braves won 93 games and finished 3 games ahead of the San Francisco Giants. Like the Mets, the Braves had top-notch pitching, led by Phil Niekro who went 23–13 and Ron Reed who went 18–10. The Braves were no pushovers, and Koosman was worried.

"Personally, I went in there a little leery because the Braves had good pitching and good hitting, and we really felt like we were the underdogs," Koosman said. "All of the writers were saying that it was going to be a pitchers' duel, but it wasn't; it was a hitter's duel. I felt we were really lucky to beat the Braves."

It was far from a pitcher's duel, in fact, as the Mets defeated the Braves 9–5, 11–6, and 7–4 to sweep the NLCS and advance to the World Series. There, the heavily favored Baltimore Orioles were waiting.

"To tell you the truth, we didn't know what to expect from the Orioles," Koosman said. "We had heard so many good things about them and how strong they were."

The Orioles were more than strong; they were the Paul Bunyan of the American League, winning 109 games during the regular season. They had power—Boog Powell (37 homers, 121 RBIs), Frank Robinson (32 homers, 100 RBIs); speed—Paul Blair (32 doubles, 20 steals); and defense—four Orioles won the Gold Glove in 1969: Brooks Robinson (third base), Davey Johnson (second base), Mark Belanger (shortstop), Paul Blair (outfield). Not to mention their pitching, led by Mike Cuellar, who went 23–11; Dave McNally, who went 20–7; and Jim Palmer, who went 16–4.

Long before the days of game films, the Mets relied on their advance scouting team to give them very specific details on every opponent that they would face.

"We had meetings where the advanced scout meets with the pitcher and goes over each hitter and how to pitch him and how to play him," Koosman said. "Then, before every game, Gil Hodges had the routine of having a meeting with Gil, the pitcher and the catcher, the center fielder, and the shortstop. We went over every hitter and how we were going to pitch to them and how we were going to play him. The shortstop ran the infield, and the center fielder ran the outfield. That was our routine before every game, and we'd go from there."

In Game One in Baltimore, it appeared the Mets did not prepare enough for Baltimore's Don Buford, who stole the show—leading off the bottom of the first with a home run blast to right field off of Tom Seaver. In the bottom of the fourth inning, after Baltimore scratched out 2 more runs against Seaver, Buford stroked a run-scoring double to right to give the Orioles a 4–0 lead. The Mets would score only 1 run in the opener, on a seventh-inning sacrifice fly. After the 4–1 loss, Koosman—who was set to start Game Two—said the Mets didn't make any specific adjustments but did have one very clear goal. "I know as a team we didn't want to go back to New York down 2 games," he said.

Jerry Koosman leaps into the arms of catcher Jerry Grote after the Mets stunned the world and won the 1969 World Series.

Koosman had a lot to say about the next day's result as it turned out, holding the powerhouse Orioles to just 1 run on two hits over 8⅔ innings. In fact, Koosman took a no-hitter into the seventh inning, before Paul Blair finally broke through with a single and later scored. However, that was the only run that Koosman surrendered, which proved to be just enough. Baltimore's Dave McNally pitched very well himself and only gave up 2 runs—a solo home run to Donn Clendenon and an RBI single to Al Weis. The Mets had done what they had set out to do and left Baltimore with a split of the first two games.

As the World Series shifted to Shea Stadium, the Mets were energized by the pitching—and hitting—of Gary Gentry and an overall balanced offensive attack. However, Game Three of the 1969 World Series would soon become known as the Tommie Agee show, first with his bat and then with his glove. Agee led off the bottom of the first inning by blasting a home run to almost dead center off of Jim Palmer. The Mets increased their lead to 3–0 when Gentry doubled in 2 runs in the bottom of the second. However, it was the Mets defense that had

Shea buzzing on this day, as Agee was about to make two of the greatest plays in World Series history and be credited with saving five runs.

The first catch came in the top of the fourth inning when the Orioles had runners on first and third. Baltimore's Elrod Hendricks drove a ball deep to left-center field, and Agee raced over from center field to make an incredible, back-handed grab just in front of the 396-mark on the fence. NBC broadcaster Curt Gowdy described the play:

> There's a drive into deep left-center, racing hard is Agee—*what a grab! Tom Agee saves 2 runs!*

In the bottom of the sixth inning, the Mets scored again to extend their lead to 4–0 thanks to a Jerry Grote run-scoring double. However, in the top of the seventh it was once again time for Agee to be the star. The Orioles loaded the bases on three-straight Gentry walks, causing the Mets manager to summon Nolan Ryan from the bullpen to face Paul Blair. It looked as though that move would backfire as Blair launched a ball to deep right-center field. It was Lindsey Nelson with the call:

> And it is a fly ball; it'll be tough to get to, Agee is going, and Agee . . . makes a diving catch—he's out!

Agee's second catch was a diving basket catch as he raced full speed from his center-field position to right-center field. The two catches definitely saved the day for the Mets, who won the game and took a 2–1 lead in the Series.

Game Four would prove to be a major tipping point in the Series, as it was a game that the Mets would absolutely have to win if they wanted to keep alive their goal of not returning to Baltimore. The game ended up featuring a brilliant pitching performance, one of the greatest catches in the history of the World Series, a controversial moment, and an error in extra innings that led to the game-winning run. Not too shabby for a single game, especially since everything on that list fell in the Mets' favor.

First, there was the brilliant pitching performance, which belonged to Tom Seaver, who bounced back from his Game One loss to pitch 10 innings, giving up just 1 run on 6 hits. Next was the catch, made by Mets right fielder Ron Swoboda. It was the top of the ninth inning, with the Mets leading 1–0. Baltimore had the tying run on third base when Brooks Robinson slammed a sinking liner into right-center field. Swoboda ranged to his right, dove headlong, and somehow snagged the ball before it hit the ground. Frank Robinson, the runner on third, would score the tying run, but had Swoboda not made the catch, who knows how far Brooks Robinson would have gotten.

"That's a do-or-die play," Swoboda told reporters after the game. "You know that if you catch the ball you're not going to throw anybody out, but you have to try. If it gets by you, OK, there's nothing you can do. You just have to take the chance you can reach the ball. . . . So I just go as far as I can and pray. If there's one chance in a thousand to catch it, I'm going to try."

The Mets did not score in the bottom of the ninth, and the game moved to the 10th inning, with Seaver remaining in the game. Baltimore got a man on and eventually pushed him to third, but Seaver struck out Paul Blair to end the threat and the inning.

That brought up the bottom of the 10th inning, the controversy, the error, and the game-winning run. Jerry Grote led off the inning with a double to left field. Al Weis was then intentionally walked. Seaver's spot in the lineup was next, and Gil Hodges sent up J. C. Martin to hit for the Mets ace. Martin squared to bunt out in front of the plate, toward first base. Baltimore relief pitcher Pete Richert pounced off of the mound and went to grab the ball at the exact same time as catcher Elrod Endricks. The two were so close to each other that they nearly collided. However, Richert grabbed the ball, possibly a little frazzled from the near-collision, turned, and fired toward first. His throw hit Martin in the wrist, though, and ricocheted toward second base. As the ball rolled away, the winning run scored for the Mets. Naturally, the play was not without controversy.

When Martin was hit with the ball, he was to the left of the foul line, technically in fair territory. The rules state that a baserunner moving from home plate to first base must remain in the running lane. Martin was not in that lane. However, the rule book states that it is within the umpire's discretion to rule whether the runner did—or did not—interfere, with the play. In the umpire's judgment, Martin did not interfere and the play—and the win—stood.

For his part, Seaver gave an objective opinion of the ruling, which allowed the Mets to prevail 2–1 and take a commanding 3–1 lead in the Series.

"I just saw it as the winning run," Seaver told reporters. "Safe at home. Definitely safe."

It had now come to this—the New York Mets, the same franchise that had lost 120 games seven seasons earlier, the same franchise that had lost more than 100 games six of their first eight seasons—were one game away from becoming champions of the World. Starting pitcher Jerry Koosman was not a part of most of those losing teams, but he most definitely was aware of what was at stake heading into that fifth game. He knew that the Mets wanted to end things right there at Shea Stadium.

"I was very aware of it, very aware of it," Koosman said. "There's no way that I, or any of my teammates, wanted to go back to Baltimore. We were going to give it our absolute best to win that game and clinch it right there in New York. We went into that game, and I was thrilled to pitch it. I wanted to pitch it."

In the top of the third inning, Mark Belanger led off with a single to right field off of Koosman. The next batter was Baltimore pitcher Dave McNally, and the Mets were ready for the bunt.

"We were playing for a bunt. So I was going to throw him a high fastball, and hopefully he would pop it up, and maybe we could get a double play," Koosman remembered. "Well, I throw the high fastball, he was swinging away, and he hit it out of the ballpark. And it just stunned us all. That was the big play, and that really kind of teed me off."

Koosman was even madder three batters later when Frank Robinson homered to left-center to give the Orioles a 3–0 lead.

"I got back to the dugout, and I was really perturbed," Koosman said. "I said, 'Guys, that's all they're going to get; they're not going to get any more. Let's go beat 'em.' And that's exactly what we did."

In the sixth inning, things got a little strange. In the top of the frame, Koosman appeared to hit Frank Robinson with a pitch, but the umpire ruled that the ball actually hit Robinson's bat and did not award the slugger first base. There was obviously no replay review in 1969, although it was clear from the replay that Robinson indeed had been hit by the pitch. Instead, he would go on to strike out. As if the Baseball Gods were having a lot of fun with this World Series, in the bottom of the sixth inning the Mets' Cleon Jones also appeared to be hit in the foot with a pitch from Dave McNally. However, once again the home-plate umpire, Lou DiMuro, said no, the ball did not hit Jones at all and instead just hit the ground. However, Jones argued, and somehow the Mets manager emerged from the dugout with the ball, showing the umpire that it had shoe polish on it from Jones's shoe. As inexplicable as that seemed, DiMuro relented after seeing this new evidence and awarded Jones first base. Baltimore manager Earl Weaver went crazy, and McNally stood to the side of the mound dumbfounded.

The next batter was Donn Clendenon, who blasted his third home run of the World Series and pulled the Mets to within 3–2. Koosman had already promised his team he wasn't going to give up any more runs, so when they tied the game in the seventh inning on Al Weis's home run and went ahead 5–3 in the bottom of the eighth inning, all Koosman had to do was retire the final three batters.

The top of the ninth started a little shaky for Koosman, who walked Frank Robinson to lead off the inning. That meant that every other hitter Koosman would face in the inning would be the potential tying run. However, the Mets lefty was able to retire the next two hitters—Boog Powell and Brooks Robinson—bringing Davey Johnson to the plate with one on and two men out.

"The moment was unbelievable," Koosman said of that final at-bat. "It was so noisy in the stadium you couldn't hear yourself think. I was basically only throwing fastballs in the ninth inning because I was so excited and nervous and I couldn't get my curveball over. I knew that from my warm-up pitches. I threw fastballs and threw them as hard as I could throw them. I was just trying to throw strikes."

As Johnson stood in, Koosman fired a ball outside. One ball, no strikes. On the next pitch Koosman poured in a fastball right over the heart of the plate for a strike. One ball, one strike. Koosman then tried to get a curve over, but left it way high and outside. Two balls, one strike. Johnson ripped into the next pitch, a high fastball on the outside corner, sending a fly ball to left.

"When he hit that ball, you couldn't hear the crack of the bat, which tells a pitcher how well the ball is hit. So when he hit that ball, I couldn't tell how far it was going to go," Koosman said. "I turned around and saw Cleon Jones going back and so many thoughts were going through my mind in just a split second. When he stopped just in front of the warning track, I knew the ball wasn't out of the ballpark."

It was during that split second that Koosman flashed back to a Game Three years earlier when he was pitching for the Auburn Mets of the New York–Penn League. Koosman had a no-hitter going with two outs in the ninth inning when Don Manning of the Binghamton Triplets sent a fly ball to right field. A no-hitter for young Jerry Koosman! It was not to be, however, as the ball clanked off of right fielder Joe Dodder's mitt. The official scorer scored the ball as a hit, and Koosman's no-no was gone.

"The right fielder dropped it, and the official scorer scored it a hit. . . . I lost the no-hitter because of a dropped fly ball," Koosman remembered more than 50 years later. At the time, the twenty-three-year-old Koosman took it all in stride.

"It was the closest I've ever come to a no-hitter, and I would have liked to get it," Koosman told reporters following the game. "That sure wasn't a very solid hit."

For his part, Dodder—who never made it past Double A—was stunned that it was scored as a hit.

"They ruled it a hit?" he yelled after the game. "That ball landed in the pocket of my glove and bounced out. It was definitely an error." Dodder should know— the following season after being moved to first base by the Dubuque Packers, the Dodgers affiliate in the Midwest League, Dodder committed 28 errors.

So as Koosman turned to watch the flight of Johnson's hit as it headed out to Cleon Jones, there was only one thought in his mind—*Catch the ball.*

"When [Cleon] squared around to catch the ball, I was saying to myself, *Cleon, catch the ball, and do not drop it.*"

Koosman had nothing to worry about, as Jones had it all the way and just in front of the warning track made the catch that will always be remembered by Mets fans.

"I turned around, and here comes Jerry Grote, and I just jumped into his arms," Koosman said. "He caught me, and it was just elation. It was like the whole weight of that Series, and all of the pressure, and all the press, everything was just relieved off your shoulders. It was like we were in heaven."

History has treated the 1969 New York Mets well. They have stood the test of time and will always be considered one of the greatest sports stories of the twentieth century. The team lives on in pop culture, having been referenced in numerous television shows, books, and movies. For Jerry Koosman, it is nothing but happy memories.

"It's really great, and I feel like a part of me is a New Yorker," said Koosman, who is originally from Minnesota. "When I am in New York, I feel a lot like I am back home again. Although no one recognizes me anymore, it's always fun to go back and reminisce. No matter who you talk to, they want to talk about the 1969 Mets and the 1969 World Series."

19

Ya Gotta Believe (1973)

On August 30, 1973, the New York Mets were where many other Mets teams had resided—last place, at 10 games under .500. Four years removed from the 1969 World Series title, the Mets had won 83 games in each of the past three seasons. That was never close enough to even sniff the postseason. Now, in 1973, it appeared that the Mets were finished heading into the final month of the season. Three weeks earlier, reliever Tug McGraw had shouted his now-famous "Ya Gotta Believe!" following a team meeting. While there may have been few believers at the time, 1973 was a strange season, and the National League East appeared to be up for grabs throughout the year.

Just three weeks later, as the Mets put together some wins and McGraw continued his battle cry, the Mets had improved their record to 77–77, which was inexplicably good enough to launch them into first place. New York closed out the season winning five of its last seven games and won the division by a game and a half—with a record of 82–79 and winning percentage of just .509.

However, in the end it really didn't matter, as the Mets were heading to face the big, bad Cincinnati Reds and their 99 victories. On paper, it was not a fair match-up.

"It was a thrill to be heading into that environment," said Mets pitcher Jon Matlack. "There was a certain amount of apprehension knowing who we had to play and an awareness about how good they were. Everybody recognized that we were playing really well at that point, and every night different guys seemed to step up and do whatever it took to accomplish a goal and ultimately win a ballgame. But we had to wonder whether that was going to continue."

In Game One of the best-of-five National League Championship Series, Cincinnati's Jack Billingham and the Mets' Tom Seaver locked up in a classic game. Seaver pitched brilliantly, giving up just 1 run on 5 hits, striking out 13, and walking none through eight innings. However, the Mets could not muster any offense, and Johnny Bench hit a walk-off homer against Seaver with one out in the bottom of the ninth inning to give the Reds a 2–1 victory and a 1–0 series lead.

"I had done the pitching chart for Game One when Tom Seaver pitched and got beat, and I remember finishing that chart and, before I turned it in, looking over it and going, 'You know what, that's about as good a ballgame as anyone can pitch,'" Matlack said. "He gave up 2 solo home runs, and we ended up losing 2–1, and I'm thinking to myself, *My God, what do I have to do tomorrow to hold these guys at bay and give us a chance to win?*"

Game Two would indeed match up Matlack, who won 14 games during the regular season, against the Reds' Don Gullett, who had won 18 games.

"There was a sense of urgency, I guess you can say, but I looked at it in a different framework in that I wanted to approach the game from a one-pitch-at-a-time, one-out-at-a-time, one-inning-at-a-time type of approach," Matlack said. "I wanted to stay in the moment and not get too far ahead of myself."

Adding to Matlack's urgency was that the Mets could ill afford to fall behind 2–0 against the Reds, who had one of the most formidable lineups in all of baseball. Names like Pete Rose, Joe Morgan, Tony Perez, and Johnny Bench littered the Cincinnati batting order.

"I don't think it's the kind of thing where you look at the notoriety of a player or his stats," Matlack said. "You have to think that this is just a guy with a bat with strengths and weaknesses, and I have to match my strengths and weaknesses against his given the situation of the game and try and win that battle. That was what I was taught to do. My thought was that I didn't want to allow a base-runner reach base. Is that realistic? Probably not, but you have to adjust, and ultimately I was just trying to keep us in the ballgame, which I was able to do."

Just prior to the start of the game, Matlack was given a little boost by his teammate—and one of the Mets' best hitters—Rusty Staub.

"Right before the game, Rusty came by me and said, 'I got Gullett's pitches. If you can keep us close, I'm going to get him before the day is over,'" Matlack remembered. "So that was kind of lingering in the back of my mind, and, of course, it ultimately came true."

In the top of the fourth inning, Staub proved he was not just giving Matlack encouragement when he ripped a Gullett offering over the fence for a home run and a 1–0 Mets lead. That would be, it turned out, all the support Matlack would need, as the 1972 Rookie of the Year completely shut down the powerful Cincinnati lineup, allowing just 2 singles in the game.

"It was definitely one of my better games—at a time where we really needed it to happen—so am I proud of that accomplishment, you're damn right I am," Matlack said. "Why the way things fell the way they did that day I really don't know, but everything seemed to be working, and we were able to get the results."

The 2 hits that Matlack surrendered were not to one of the many future Hall of Famers who batted for the Reds that day, but instead both came off the bat of Andy Kosco. Throughout the entire 1973 season, Kosco managed just 33 hits in 47 games played.

"I don't know why Sparky [Anderson] had to put Kosco in the lineup that day, but he did; otherwise, I might have had something even better," Matlack said with a laugh.

The Mets—behind Matlack's performance—won the game 5–0 and tied the NLCS at 1–1.

Although the Mets would win Game Three at Shea Stadium to take a 2–1 lead in the series, that game is best known for the fight between Pete Rose and Bud Harrelson. The melee took place when Rose slid hard into second base against the Mets shortstop; however, it really began one day earlier. According to Cincinnati second baseman Joe Morgan, Rose was ticked off that Harrelson had been critical of the way the Reds played in their Game Two loss. So when Rose had the opportunity to try to take out Harrelson on a double-play ball in the fifth inning, he did—and words were exchanged, and the benches emptied. It wasn't much of a baseball fight, but it got the fans at Shea riled up—and Rose was pelted with various items when he went out to his left-field position the following inning.

The rowdiness got so bad that the National League threatened to declare a forfeit by the Mets, prompting manager Yogi Berra and several players—big names such as Seaver, Mays, and Staub—to walk out toward left field and ask the fans to stop throwing debris.

Pitcher Jon Matlack was a key to the Mets' success in 1973.

"I went into the dugout and asked Yogi and Willie Mays to come out and talk to the fans," National League President Charles "Chub" Feeney told reporters after the game. "They'll recognize Willie, but if I went out there, they'd probably throw things at me."

The Mets fans listened and behaved, and the Mets went on to win the game by a score of 9–2. However, the Reds scratched back to win Game Four, 2–1 in 12 innings, and the NLCS went to a deciding Game Five.

Luckily for the Mets, they had ace Tom Seaver heading back to the mound for the decisive game. Just four days earlier, Seaver had pitched one of the best games of his career, only to end up on the short end of a 2–1 decision. Surely that could not—and would not—happen twice in a series. It didn't. Seaver pitched well again, surrendering just 1 earned run in eight-plus innings of work, and this time got plenty of offensive support from his squad, as the Mets won 7–2 and took the National League pennant. Here was how Mets broadcaster Lindsey Nelson called that moment:

Tug McGraw gets the sign, goes into the motion, and here's the two-strike pitch—swung on, hit on the ground toward first, Milner has the ball, flips to McGraw. It's *over. The New York Mets have won the pennant! The New York Mets have won the pennant! The New York Mets have won the pennant*—and this is a wild scene!

"To this day, it is one of the most exhilarating feelings and experiences that I had in the sport," Matlack said. "That's why we all play—to ultimately make it to the World Series—and I am very, very pleased that we were able to accomplish that. If you look back, every club in our division was in first place at some point during the season, and we were fortunate enough to take our turn at the end when it counted."

The only thing that stands out as a negative for Matlack is the fact that the Mets lost the subsequent World Series to the Oakland Athletics. Despite the fact that Oakland was heavily favored, the Mets had managed a 3–2 series lead and appeared to have the upper hand.

"Should we have won the World Series? In my mind, absolutely," Matlack said. "The A's never showed up until Game Seven. We literally should have won every one of the first six games and somehow lost three of them. The opportunity was there, and we weren't able to seize it. It just got away from us."

However, make no mistake—losing the World Series does nothing to lessen the pride Matlack feels about winning the 1973 National League pennant.

"It was a hell of an accomplishment," he said proudly.

Part Two

20

The Kid Beats Kerfeld (1986)

The Mets and Houston Astros were embroiled in one of the greatest postseason games in history on October 14, 1986, when Mets catcher Gary Carter stepped to the plate to face Astros reliever Charlie Kerfeld in the bottom of the 12th inning with the game tied at 1–1. The NLCS was also tied at that moment, with each team having won 2 games. The winner of Game Five would hold the upper hand heading back to the Astrodome for Game Six, and potentially Game Seven. However, the game might have meant more to the Mets, who wanted no part of Houston ace Mike Scott in a potential Game 7. If the Mets could pull out Game Five, they would, at the very least, control their own destiny as to whether they had to face Scott one more time.

Through the first 11 innings, it was an epic matchup between starting pitchers Dwight Gooden of the Mets and Nolan Ryan of the Astros. Each starter had allowed just 1 run—Ryan in nine innings pitched, Gooden in 10. However, the starters were now out, and the game was in the hands of the relievers. Jesse Orosco had shut down the Astros for two innings, and Kerfeld had done the same for his squad. Now, in the bottom of the 12th inning, Kerfeld was starting his third inning of work.

After getting Lenny Dykstra to ground out to the first baseman, Wally Backman singled into left field. Keith Hernandez was now the batter. However, everything changed when Kerfeld attempted to pick Backman off first base. The throw was wild and Backman scampered to second. Houston manager Hal

Lanier decided to walk Hernandez to face a struggling Gary Carter instead. The perennial All-Star had gotten just 1 hit in 21 at-bats in the NLCS—an embarrassing .048 batting average—and he was feeling the pressure. However, what some might not have forgotten by then, but what Carter most certainly did not, is Kerfeld's interaction with Carter three days earlier.

In Game Three of the Series, Carter was just 1-for-12 in the Series. The Mets and Astros had split the first two games. So there was Carter, facing a young, somewhat zany pitcher by the name of Charlie Kerfeld. Known for doing quirky spins, twirls, and hops on the mound, Kerfeld was the kind of pitcher that opponents—and their fans—learned quickly to despise. He was not as vile as someone like John Rocker would eventually be, but he had no trouble getting under the skin of others.

For the Mets and their fans, a negative feeling about Kerfeld was solidified forever when the fireballer induced Carter to ground back to the mound for an easy out in the bottom of the eighth inning of Game Three. Instead of simply making the play—an impressive behind-the-back stab of Carter's comebacker— Kerfeld snagged the ball, extending his arm toward Carter, showing the All-Star the ball in a taunting fashion, before tossing it to first base. He was clearly mocking the struggling Carter.

"You just don't embarrass an All-Star and future Hall of Famer like that," said Mets broadcaster Howie Rose.

When asked about the play after the game, Carter told reporters he wasn't sure what Kerfeld was thinking by pointing the ball in his direction.

"I don't know. You read things and hear things about the crazy life of Charlie Kerfeld, maybe it *was* innocent," Carter said. "He caught the ball behind his back, and maybe it surprised him. But there are certain things you've got to be careful not to do to an opposing player, and pointing fingers is one of them."

According to Rose, that taunt most definitely had to be "somewhere in Carter's mind" when he stepped up to face Kerfeld three days later with Game Five on the line.

"I kept telling myself, *I'm going to come through here*. I knew it was just a matter of time. I'm not an .050 hitter," Carter told reporters after the game.

Once again, Kerfeld stood atop the mound and stared down Carter, who worked the count to 3 balls and 2 strikes. When the first 3–2 pitch was on its way, Backman and Hernandez took off, as runners tend to do on a 3–2 pitch with

Part Two

The Mets had their rally hats on, as Game 5 against the Astros went into extra innings.

a contact hitter at the plate. Carter fouled back a high and tight pitch—which might have been out of the strike zone.

"When the runners were going, the fastball that I fouled off was up and in. It might've even been a ball," Carter said after the game. "In that situation, no way I was going to get called out on strikes, so I swung at it."

On the next 3–2 pitch, manager Davey Johnson decided to not have the runners on the move, fearing that might have been a distraction to Carter. No matter, as the Mets catcher rifled Kerfeld's fastball back through the mound on a line. However, this time it was a smash that the Houston pitcher had no chance to grab—forward or backward. "It was down a little, a bit more in the strike zone," Carter told reporters, "and over the middle of the plate."

Mets radio voice Bob Murphy described the action:

And a groundball—base hit through the middle. Backman around third, Backman coming home, the throw—he *scores!* The Mets *win!*

Backman scored easily. The Mets won the game and in doing so took a critical 3–2 lead in the Series. All of a sudden, Carter's slump didn't seem all that important.

Gary Carter throws his arms into the air in celebration of the Mets' victory in Game Five of the 1986 NLCS.

"It was an enormous hit, and if it's not Gary's signature moment with the Mets, it's got to be right up there," Rose said. "It was a very integral hit in them winning the pennant and then ultimately winning the World Series."

For his part, following the loss, Kerfeld was direct with reporters.

"I've faced Gary a lot this year, and that's the first time he's got a hit off me," he said. "I challenged Gary, and he beat me. He won the bet."

As the ball got through the infield, Carter—from just beyond the batter's box—extended both arms, fists to the sky in celebration.

"He threw his arms up, and I'm sure he felt like there was a huge weight lifted off of his shoulders and at the same time gave the Mets a desperately needed win going back to Houston," Rose said. "What that hit meant, apart from the obvious—which was putting them one win away from a pennant—was that it gave them control of the 'avoid Mike Scott at all costs' destiny."

If only Game Six ended up being that simple.

21

Mets Slay the Astros (1986)

When is a Game Six really a Game Seven? When the pitcher you will be facing in that Game Seven has defeated you mentally before he ever climbs the mound. And it was no secret. Prior to the game, when meeting with reporters, Mets manager Davey Johnson was about as honest as a manager could possibly be.

"It's very simple," Johnson told reporters. "If we win the sixth game, we don't have to think about Scott in the seventh game."

Mike Scott—the Astros' ace right-hander who had dominated the Mets in Games One and Four of the League Championship Series, was 18–10 on the season, with a 2.22 earned-run average. That was also the same Mike Scott who had pitched a no-hitter in the game in which the Astros clinched the National League Western Division—the same Mike Scott who pitched for the Mets from 1979 through 1982, winning a combined 14 games over four seasons. He was the same Mike Scott that was traded following the 1982 season for outfielder Danny Heep (in this case, Scott was the same guy but a different pitcher).

In Game One of the NLCS, Scott pitched a 5-hit shutout against the Mets, striking out 14 and walking only 1. In Game Four, Scott pitched a complete game, scattering 3 hits and giving up 1 run. Along the way, the Mets were convinced Scott was either scuffing or otherwise doctoring the ball, and they publicly voiced their concerns. The complaints were largely dismissed, and the Mets were thought to be whining because they could not touch anything Scott was throwing up to the plate. One of the Mets who spoke out loudest against Scott was Gary Carter, who had caught Scott in the All-Star Game earlier that season and said the balls he was throwing were definitely altered—scratched to allow them to have a greater drop.

"I haven't seen Mike Scott get caught," Houston manager Hal Lanier told reporters. "If they can get away with it, let them get away with it."

The fact was, it didn't really matter how much the Mets complained about Scott; he was looming for Game Seven unless the Mets could end the LCS in Game Six.

"We will never know, but Scott was in their heads," Mets broadcaster Howie Rose said. "Everyone really approached it with the incredible desperation of a Game Seven."

If the must-win had permeated the Mets dugout, imagine what it was doing to Mets fans.

"I don't think there's any doubt about it," said baseball reporter Ed Randall, who was covering both the National League Championship Series and American League Championship Series in 1986, "every Mets fan I speak to of a certain age admits that if the Mets had not won Game Six there was no way that they were going to win Game Seven because Scott was inside their heads."

How could the game itself possibly surpass the build-up? Well, you extend the game from nine to 16 innings and include one of the most nail-biting endings in baseball history. Check.

"Houston was scary because they had pitching and they had guys who were really hot," said Mets All-Star Howard Johnson. "We were definitely the two best teams in the league. I can't put my finger on it, but it just seemed like we were destined to win it."

If that was the Mets' destiny, then it didn't seem that way early on, as the Astros jumped out to a quick 3–0 lead in the bottom of the first inning. In that frame, Mets starter Bob Ojeda—who led the team with 18 victories in 1986— got touched up for 3 runs on 4 hits, including run-scoring hits by Phil Garner, Glenn Davis, and José Cruz. With the way that Houston starter Bob Knepper was pitching, those 3 runs looked like more than enough. Knepper had given up just 2 singles over the first eight innings to the Mets, and it seemed like Game Seven was meant to be.

Then, the Mets broke through in the top of ninth inning and started to chip away at Knepper and the Astros.

"To me it just typified the season we had," Johnson said. "I thought we had the better team, but the guy who was on the mound for them that day, Bob Knepper, he always seemed to handle us pretty well. In typical Mets fashion, the guys just kind of strung hits together, tied it up, and it happened so quickly I don't think Houston even realized what was happening to them."

It did happen quickly. Lenny Dykstra led off the ninth inning by flicking a fly-ball triple to center field, which was followed by Mookie Wilson's RBI single. The Mets were on the board. After Kevin Mitchell grounded out to third base, advancing Wilson to second, Keith Hernandez stepped to the plate against Knepper and ripped a fly-ball double off the center-field fence, scoring Wilson. That was it for the unhittable Bob Knepper, who was replaced by Houston closer Dave Smith.

The first batter Smith faced was Gary Carter, who fought back from a 2–2 count to walk. Smith threw seven-straight fastballs to Carter, staying away from his trademark forkball, setting up a matchup with slugger Darryl Strawberry. After slamming a ball deep down the right-field line, but well foul, Strawberry too walked to load the bases. Ray Knight then hit one of the most important sacrifice fly balls in Mets history when he sent a ball to right field. Hernandez scored easily, doing a little hop as he reached the plate. The game was tied, 3–3.

The marathon was just beginning, as the Mets and Astros battled on for four more scoreless innings. At one point ABC-TV, which was carrying the game, showed Mike Scott sitting in the dugout.

"Mike Scott can't do a thing about it," announcer Keith Jackson told the television audience, "except hope he gets a chance tomorrow night."

The Mets were trying their hardest to not have a tomorrow night. The game remained tied until the top of the 14th inning, when the Mets took a 4–3 lead on Wally Backman's RBI single off of Houston's Aurelio López. The Mets were now just three outs away from advancing to the World Series. However, Houston's Billy Hatcher had other ideas. With one out in the bottom of the 14th inning, Hatcher hit a ball off of the left-field foul pole off Jesse Orosco, and the game, once again, was tied. It remained that way though the 15th inning as well.

"I think that was probably the most incredibly tense baseball game I have ever seen," Rose said. "For eight innings, nothing much happened. Really, it was from the ninth inning on that it took on the timber that it did. I think there have been a lot of great games that I have seen over the years, but I don't know that you can have more of a sustained tension and nervousness than what existed in that Game Six, especially considering what potentially loomed in Game Seven. In retrospect, it was delightfully tortuous, but in real time it was baseball torture of the highest magnitude."

The Mets seemingly ended the torture in the top of the 16th inning when they scored 3 runs on 3 hits to take a 7–4 lead. However, the Astros once again fought back to score two runs in the bottom of the 16th inning. Finally, with two outs, the tying run on second base and potential winning run on first base, Orosco struck out Kevin Bass, ending one of the most exciting games in baseball history and sending the Mets to the World Series for the third time in franchise history.

Bob Murphy made this historic call on WHN radio:

Swing and a miss! Swing and a miss! Struck him out! Struck him out! The Mets are going to the World Series!

Despite Game Six of the 1986 National League Championship Series being one of the greatest postseason games ever, many baseball fans seem to forget that it even took place. Instead, the 1986 Mets often are defined by a baseball

The Mets celebrate after winning the 1986 National League pennant.

rolling through a certain first baseman's legs. However, this was a Mets team that won 108 games during the regular season and defeated an upstart Houston team in an incredible six-game series.

"The series between New York and Houston was just incredible," Randall said. "Without a doubt, I think the memory fades when it comes to the NLCS from 1986 because the World Series that followed was one for the ages."

The Mets would now advance to face the Boston Red Sox, who themselves had just gone through an emotional series win against the California Angels.

"Through the passage of time, a lot of people seem to forget how special the 1986 postseason was," Randall said. "I can't remember when both the American League Championship Series and National League Championship Series were so compelling simultaneously. Both series were incredible, and that is why that was probably the greatest postseason ever."

Part Two

22

Game Six (1986)

No one had a better view than Howard Johnson.

On October 25, 55,078 people packed into Shea Stadium to watch Game Six of the 1986 World Series between the Mets and Boston Red Sox. Over time, that number has grown to fictional heights, as just about every Mets fan that you run into claims to have been at the game.

Had it not been for Game Six of the 1986 World Series, Game Six of the 1986 National League Championship Series against the Houston Astros would have been the most talked-about Game Six in franchise history. The truth is, all too often Game Six of the NLCS is forgotten thanks to the baseball contest that will forever be known to all Mets fans simply as "Game Six."

The fact that the Mets were even playing in a Game Six was a testament to the team's never-say-die attitude. Having lost the first two games of the fall classic at Shea Stadium, the Mets traveled to Boston's Fenway Park in the worst-case scenario. However, in Game Three Lenny Dykstra led off the game against Dennis "Oil Can" Boyd with a home run into the right-field corner, and the Mets were on their way. Later in the inning, Gary Carter drove in 2 runs with a booming double to center field, and the Mets never looked back, winning the game by a score of 7–1. The next night, Carter homered twice over the Green Monster, and Dykstra hit another, as the Mets drew even in the Series with a 6–2 win. In the pivotal Game Five, Dwight Gooden was chased from the game after giving up 4 runs on 9 hits in just four innings. The Mets could not muster any of the offense they had had in the previous two nights, and the Red Sox won the game 4–2. Boston was now one win away from winning its first World Series since 1918. New York, meanwhile, was one loss away from squandering one of the greatest seasons in franchise history. It was time for Game Six.

While every Mets fan remembers how Game Six ended, few remember how it began—or really anything that happened before the 10th inning. Boston sent its ace Roger Clemens to the mound in hopes he could deliver a championship performance. It wasn't really asking anything too tough, as during the regular season Clemens went 24–4 with a 2.48 earned-run average and 238 strikeouts. He was an All-Star, won the American League Cy Young Award, and was named the American League Most Valuable Player. The Mets, for their part, turned to their top pitcher in 1986, Bobby Ojeda, who went 18–5 with a 2.57 earned run average.

The Red Sox jumped out to a quick 2–0 lead in the game, scoring runs in the first and second innings. The Mets tied the game in the bottom of the fifth on a Ray Knight run-scoring hit and a Danny Heep double play, which scored a run. Each team would add a run, and after eight innings the game was tied at 3–3.

After the Red Sox failed to score in the top of the ninth inning, it appeared that the Mets might pull off the victory in the bottom of the ninth. After Knight led off the inning with a walk, Mookie Wilson dropped down a bunt in front of the plate that was grabbed by catcher Rich Gedman (remember that name!), who picked the ball up and fired it wildly toward second base. The throw was wide of the base, Knight was safe at second, and Wilson was safe at first—two on, no out. The next batter was Howard Johnson, who the entire stadium assumed was going to bunt. He didn't and instead struck out. The next two hitters—Lee Mazzilli and Lenny Dykstra—flew out to left field. The Mets, it seemed, missed a golden opportunity to win the game and instead headed to the 10th inning.

In the top of the 10th, Dave Henderson led off for the Red Sox and blasted a home run over the left-field fence. Every Mets fan felt their heart fall into their stomach. Four batters later, Marty Barrett singled home Wade Boggs for an all-important insurance run and a 5–3 Boston lead. It was time to roll in the champagne and cover the lockers with plastic. The Red Sox were three outs away from winning their long-elusive championship.

Calvin Schiraldi, who had pitched the eighth and ninth innings for the Red Sox, returned to the mound to close the Mets out in the bottom of the 10th.

Part Two

Schiraldi was no stranger to the mound at Shea. During the two previous seasons, he had little success throwing from that same mound as a member of the Mets in 1984 and 1985. He was traded following the 1985 season for the Mets' Game Six starter—Bob Ojeda. There was no mushy reunion here, though. Schiraldi was looking to deal the death blow to the franchise that had given up on him.

As quickly as the inning started, Schiraldi had gotten two outs—the first on Wally Backman's fly ball to left fielder Jim Rice and the second on Keith Hernandez's fly ball to left-center that Henderson caught. As Henderson made the catch and threw the ball back into the infield, he could not help but let a smirk appear on his face. Why not? He was about to be a World Series champion and a World Series hero.

Whoever was running the large color scoreboard at Shea—the one Mets fans always affectionately referred to as Diamond Vision—got a little overanxious, hit a button, and "Congratulations Boston Red Sox, 1986 World Champions" appeared briefly.

Then, it happened.

The batter was Gary Carter—single. The next batter was Kevin Mitchell—single, Carter to second. The next batter was Ray Knight—single, Carter scored to make it 5–4, and Mitchell moved to third. Boston manager John McNamara then decided to change pitchers and called Bob Stanley in from the bullpen. The next batter was Mookie Wilson—and no one had a better view of the at-bat than Howard Johnson.

"Being on deck," Johnson said. "I really got to see everything up close. It was unbelievable."

Vin Scully, already a legendary baseball voice in 1986, was at the microphone for NBC-TV for the game:

It's up to Bob Stanley, and it's up to Mookie Wilson, and the crowd is alive again.

Mitchell was the tying run—90 feet away—and Knight was the potential winning run at first, as Wilson's at-bat began. After working the count to 2–2, fouling off some tough pitches along the way, what happened with Stanley's next delivery was described by Mets radio announcer Bob Murphy on WHN:

Gets away, gets away, here comes Mitchell, here comes Mitchell, tie game, tie game!

A dejected Bill Buckner walks off the field at Shea and into the history books forever.

Murphy, of course, was describing the fact that Stanley had unleashed a pitch low and inside, which eluded catcher Rich Gedman—and Wilson, who jumped out of the way of the ball—and went to the backstop. Mitchell sprinted in from third base to score the tying run, and Knight moved up to second base. As Shea Stadium exploded, Johnson had a very clear realization.

"Once that happened, I had a real strong feeling that we were going to win," Johnson said. "As soon as I saw the ball almost hit Mookie in the feet and it got by Gedman pretty fast, at that point it was really an easy run for Mitch to score. Once we tied the game up, all of the air went out of their sails—you could just feel the whole thing change. I felt really strongly that we were going to score and win. I thought Mookie would get a base hit or do something to hit the ball hard. In any event, I knew I had to be ready; I knew Bob Stanley and was really just preparing for an AB."

As Wilson's at-bat continued, Johnson was getting ready from the on-deck circle for his turn at bat, although he began to be convinced he would not get the opportunity.

"Bob Stanley was in the game, and he was a guy that I had faced before and liked facing, so I was just preparing mentally for that," Johnson said. "But it seemed like the more balls that Mookie fouled off and stayed alive, the more likely it was that he was going to get a base hit."

The at-bat went on—foul ball, followed by another foul ball—and then, finally a slow grounder toward Boston first baseman Bill Buckner. Game over.

"Oh my gosh, it was pretty incredible," Johnson said. "After all of these years you look back on it and how quickly it happened, and it's really striking. That's the one thing I always tell people when they ask me about that inning: 'You would not believe how quickly it all happened.' Two outs and then bam-bam-bam, we score three runs. It was just unreal."

Johnson vividly remembers watching the grounder from his perspective, just about 10 feet from home plate.

"I remember it very clearly," Johnson said. "Shea had a tough infield. The dirt could be bad at times, and it was late in the game, and it was kind of chewed up. I saw the ball hit, and because he got jammed it wasn't hit very hard. But it was bouncing funny, and when Buckner went to get the ball he was kind of on his heels and never really got into the right position. I always remembered that Buddy Harrelson used to tell me, 'On this infield, you field with your feet and be aggressive.' And he was decidedly not aggressive on that groundball. When it got to him, you could just see that in-between hop and get underneath his glove. I almost expected it to go under his glove because I had seen that groundball so many times."

Whether it is Scully on TV, or Murphy on radio, the calls themselves have become legendary:

Scully: Little roller up along first, *behind the bag! It gets through Buckner! Here comes Knight, and the Mets win it!*

Murphy: And a groundball trickling, it is a fair ball, it *gets by Buckner, rounding third Knight! The Mets will win the ballgame! The Mets win!*

When viewing the replay from the right-field camera and behind Buckner, you can see Johnson in the on-deck circle jump about as high as a person can jump, his bat flying.

"When I see that video it still gives me goosebumps," Johnson said. "I just threw the bat up in the air and jumped as high as I could. At that point, it was just a total release of emotion."

If Howard Johnson had the best seat in the house for Mookie Wilson's fateful groundball, then baseball reporter Ed Randall undoubtedly had the worst.

"We had a small color TV in the corner of the old Jets locker room," Randall recalled. "When the ball went through Buckner's legs, we thought the stadium was going to come down on top of us."

For Randall, being cramped in the corner of an old football locker room was just part of doing his job.

"In the top of the 10th inning, I was sitting in the auxiliary press box in right field and I remember vividly watching David Henderson hitting the home run off of Rick Aguilera," Randall said. "A friend of mine of mine from the Associated Press had said, 'That's one out,' and I remember saying, 'No, I think that's going to be gone.' And it went off the *Newsday* sign. Then, when the Red Sox scored the second run of the inning, all of us got up and started to go downstairs to the old Jets locker room and wait until the game was over and be a part of the press conference. There were thousands of fans already on the ramps, and it took a long time to get downstairs. By the time I got downstairs, it was the bottom of the 10th inning."

The Mets victory tied the 1986 World Series at 3–3—and Game Six would become something of legend. The visitors' clubhouse staff at Shea managed to get all of the bottles of champagne, plastic locker coverings—and the World Series trophy—out of the Boston locker room before any of the Red Sox made their way from the dugout.

Part Two

The Mets mob Mookie Wilson, while celebrating their Game Six victory over the Red Sox.

Johnson, who had the view of a lifetime, of course never had the chance to take that big at-bat against Bob Stanley. He is sure that Wilson would have beaten Buckner to the bag regardless, which would have put him up at bat with men on first and third and two outs. It was an at-bat he was ready for and has even allowed himself to visualize.

"I think about that often when people want to talk about that inning," Johnson said. "I think about Stanley and that I had faced him before and kind of knew what to expect. I think about what it would look like. All of those things are pretty fresh. There was no time to have a lapse in concentration. I just remember being locked in. Those are memories that don't go away very easily."

For Mets fans, the memory of Game Six will remain for eternity.

23

Mets Win It All! (1986)

The day after the Mets won Game Six of the 1986 World Series, it was 53 degrees and raining in New York City, and Game Seven would be not be played as scheduled. Could that, in any way, slow the momentum that the Mets had gained after winning Game Six in the way that they had? Some thought it was a possibility.

"I thought that the rainout really made it a tossup for Game Seven," said baseball reporter Ed Randall. "I thought with the rain, perhaps the Red Sox could regroup and that Bruce Hurst would pitch a great game, and they could absolutely win."

Randall was referring to the fact that with the extra day of rest, Boston could now decide to skip Dennis "Oil Can" Boyd, who was scheduled to start, and instead go with Hurst, who was the main man behind Roger Clemens in the rotation. And in fact, that is exactly what the Red Sox did.

However, for Mets third baseman Howard Johnson, it didn't matter who pitched, or where or when the game was played.

"To win Game Six the way we did, Game Seven was a formality," Johnson said. "[The rainout] didn't even enter our minds. We knew we were going to win Game Seven regardless of whenever we played it. It was just a feeling that we knew we were going to get the job done and finish it off."

That was the 1986 Mets in a nutshell, a confident group that set out in spring training to accomplish one goal—win it all. During the regular season, few obstacles got in their way, as the Mets won a franchise-best 108 games and cruised through the summer, winning the division by 21½ games. After surviving a scare in the National League Championship Series against the Astros, the Mets once again found themselves playing for their baseball lives in the World Series. First, they were down 2–0 heading to Boston, and then they were down 3–2. With their backs so far up against the wall in Game Six that they were all getting splinters, somehow they found a way, via a string of hits, a wild pitch, a groundball, and an aging infielder who made the mistake of a lifetime. So when the Mets fell behind 3–0 in Game Seven, no one on the bench was all that concerned.

"We felt that the whole series had turned a corner and that we had command," Johnson said. "We felt good, even being down 3–0."

The Red Sox jumped out to that 3–0 lead thanks to a strong second inning, during which Dwight Evans and Rich Gedman each hit solo home runs and Wade Boggs had a run-scoring single. The following inning, the Mets replaced starter Ron Darling with Sid Fernandez, who gave the Mets some energy, as well as perfection on the mound for the fifth and sixth innings.

In the bottom of the sixth, the Mets tied the game when Tim Teufel drew a walk to load the bases, Keith Hernandez singled in two runs, and Gary Carter followed with an RBI forceout. The game was now tied, 3–3. Then, when the Mets came to bat in the bottom of the seventh, they were staring directly at Calvin Schiraldi, the same pitcher who had struggled to close out Game Six. He found no more success in Game Seven.

Ray Knight led off the bottom of the seventh with a home run to left field to give the Mets their first lead of the night. The Mets pushed across two more runs in the frame and led after seven innings by a score of 6–3. The fat lady was warming up her vocal chords.

After the Red Sox scored two runs in the top of the eighth inning to make the score 6–5, Darryl Strawberry blasted a mammoth home run to make it 7–5. Later in the inning, Jesse Orosco—of all people—gave the Mets their final insurance run of the season with a base hit. However, Orosco had a little more work to do in the top of the ninth.

After retiring Ed Romero on a foul pop-up to first and Wade Boggs on a groundout to second, Orosco climbed the mound at Shea to do what only one other Met had ever done—gotten the final out of the World Series. Orosco, ironically, was traded for that other man—Jerry Koosman—in 1979. Ten years before

The Mets celebrate after winning the 1986 World Series.

the trade, Koosman stood on that same mound and delivered the final pitch to win a world championship. Since then, nobody else had done it. So, for Koosman, there was a definitely a connection between himself and the 1986 Mets.

"I looked at it as if it was still the left-handed energy from me since we were traded for each other," Koosman said. "I still felt such a part of that '86 season because of the trade. Plus, Jesse is a great guy. You couldn't have a better guy to have on the mound for the end of that series."

As Marty Barrett waved at the final pitch of the 1986 World Series and Jesse Orosco jumped toward the heavens, the Mets exhaled. They had done what only one other Mets team throughout history had ever done—they were world champions.

"It was just incredible," Johnson said. "It was pretty special, and it was crazy. What a celebration that was."

As time has passed, the 1986 World Series has come to be known as one of the greatest in history—maybe not for Red Sox fans, but that's a small detail.

"Given what happened in Game Six with Bill Buckner, it will always have a special place because of the gravity and timing of the error," Randall said. "Certainly when you talk about the top World Series, certainly in modern times, that one ranks right up there."

24

Leiter's Gem (1999)

You're correct—the moment I am going to discuss in this chapter is not actually a postseason moment. However, technically it is. Huh? Okay, let me explain. At the end of the 1999 season, the Mets and Cincinnati Reds were tied with identical 96–66 records. Neither was good enough to win their respective division, but both were good enough to qualify to become the National League wild-card team. The wild-card system was put in place following the 1993 season, when the two leagues went to a three-division format. The three divisional champions advanced to the postseason, as did the team with the next-best record in the league. Since the Mets and Reds finished the 1999 season tied, they had to have a one-game playoff to decide which team would move on. If you are being technical, the game counted as the 163rd game of the regular season, not a playoff game. However, since it was, in fact, after the "regular" season, I decided to put it in the postseason section of this book.

★ ★ ★

In the spring of 1987, Steve George was hanging on to his major league dream by a thread, having been in the New York Yankees' system since 1982. The fact was, this was going to be George's final season in professional baseball. Al Leiter, on the other hand, was one of the hottest young pitching prospects in the Yankees' organization. So when Topps was rushing to release their 1987 baseball-card set, they wanted to be sure to include Leiter as one of their Future Stars.

According to longtime Topps employee Butch Jacobs, who spoke to writer George Vrechek in an exclusive interview with *Sports Collectors Digest*, he was thrilled after searching through hundreds of photos to find that he had a shot of Leiter. The photos were not labeled, but "the clue that Jacobs used was that the player's glove had Leiter's uniform number 56 written on it." There was just one problem—it was not a *56* at all—it was an *SG*, and Topps ended up printing and

The Mets mob pitcher Al Leiter after advancing to the 1999 postseason.

distributing the Al Leiter rookie card with a photo of Steve George—who did look remarkably like a young Leiter. Topps realized their mistake and printed a revised version of the card. However, the market was already flooded with the Leiter card depicting George—who was out of baseball after 1987.

It was an ominous start, but the southpaw ended up with the last laugh—as he usually did. Leiter pitched in the majors for 19 seasons, threw a no-hitter, was named to two All-Star teams, and pitched in three World Series for three different teams. By far, Leiter had his greatest success in the majors during his seven seasons with the Mets—the team he grew up rooting for. While 1999 was not his greatest statistical season in New York, that was the year during which he pitched his most memorable game.

With the Mets and Reds in a flat-footed tie at the end of the regular season, the two teams would play one game for the right to play in the postseason. Thanks to a coin flip, the game would be played at Cincinnati's Cinergy Field. The way Leiter pitched, however, the game could have been played on a sandlot—or on Mars. He was that good.

The Mets jumped out to an immediate 2–0 lead in the top of the first inning when Rickey Henderson led off with a single against the Reds' Steve Parris, followed by an Edgardo Alfonzo 2-run home run. That was all Leiter would need, although he would get some more. The Mets scored single runs in the third, fifth, and sixth innings to take a commanding 5–0 lead. Leiter, meanwhile, was brilliant—scattering just 2 hits over nine innings. His shutout marked the first time in 1999 that Leiter pitched a complete game and immediately went down as one of the most clutch performances in Mets history by a pitcher.

"It seems like we've been playing must-win games for the last two weeks," Leiter told reporters following the game. "I went out with the intention of just making pitches, one by one, one after another, and I was focused in the way I'd liked to be. . . . This is something special."

Following the game, all of the accolades were heaped upon a deserving Leiter.

"Al has pitched a no-hitter," Mets manager Bobby Valentine told reporters, "but I don't know if he's ever pitched a better game."

One of Leiter's fellow pitchers on the Mets staff—veteran pitcher Orel Hershiser—spoke to Leiter during the game and gave him encouragement.

"I told him, 'You've got great stuff; go after them,'" Hershiser told reporters. "And he gave me a sort of smile that said he understood how good he was throwing, and he was so locked in nobody had to talk to him for the rest of the night."

Leiter acknowledged that he gained confidence as the game moved along.

"I knew I had something special going when they started swinging at a lot of my sliders and hitting them way foul," he told reporters after the game. "I had a couple called strikes on my curveball. You started getting in that rhythm where you get a good feel."

Even the Reds had to tip their cap to the man who had just shut them down. When asked if his team was fatigued heading into the game, Cincinnati manager Jack McKeon stated, "That didn't have anything to do with it. Al Leiter did."

Perhaps the greatest compliment the Mets received after the victory came from Reds future Hall of Famer Barry Larkin, who said, "If they play like they did tonight, I think they're going to go deep into the playoffs."

25

Pratt's Walk-Off (1999)

Steve Finley was known for his leaping grabs in center field during his Major League Baseball career in Baltimore, Houston, San Diego, Arizona, Los Angeles, San Francisco, and Colorado. He won a Gold Glove in 1995, 1996, 1999, and 2000. However, after 1999 Finley would forever be remembered by two franchises for the ball that he couldn't quite get to.

"I saw Steve starting to plan for his jump, and we have all seen it a million times on the highlight films—Steve bringing back balls," Mets catcher Todd Pratt told reporters after the game. "He went up, and I lost the ball, kind of paused. I thought he had the ball, actually. Then he put his head down. I didn't see the umpire, but [Finley] put his head down."

It was the most important game of the season for the Mets and Arizona Diamondbacks—Game Four of the National League Divisional Series. The Mets, who were leading the series 2–1, were one victory away from advancing to the National League Championship Series. The Diamondbacks needed a win to stay alive. The last person who expected to be interviewed after the game, in any capacity, was Pratt.

Pratt, a career backup catcher, was in his third season with the Mets in 1999, occasionally spelling Mike Piazza. Pratt appeared in 71 games during the regular season, batting a respectable .293 in his 160 plate appearances. He was not, however, a power threat. Pratt homered just three times in 1999, and just 16 times in his then seven years in the majors.

Heading into the postseason, there was little reason to believe Pratt would get much playing time. He was, after all, playing behind Piazza, who had batted .303, with 40 home runs and 124 runs batted in during his first full season as a member of the Mets. However, between Game Two and Game Three of the NLDS against the Diamondbacks, Piazza really was feeling the effects of the beating he had taken behind the plate all season. Specifically, the Mets star was nursing an injury to his left thumb that he had sustained late in the regular season.

Between Games Two and Three, Piazza had a bad reaction to a cortisone injection, causing his hand to swell and forcing him to the bench. In Game Three, Pratt went 0-for-2, walked a couple of times, and scored a run in the Mets' 9–2 drubbing of the Diamondbacks. The big question was, would Piazza be able to make his Shea Stadium playoff debut for Game Four, with the Mets on the verge of advancing to the National League Championship Series?

"I'm going to do everything possible to get on the diamond," Piazza told reporters the night before Game Four. "I mean, that's where I want to be. Obviously I'm going to see how it does feel in the evening and tomorrow morning. But obviously, this is a pretty critical area for a catcher. I'm very disappointed right now."

However, after not feeling he was where he should be in order to compete at the highest level, Piazza was forced to remain on the bench for the second-straight playoff game. The thirty-two-year-old Pratt was called upon again to spell the perennial All-Star catcher. Pratt struggled at the plate throughout Game Four, going 0-for-4, making outs the last three times with runners in scoring position. The Mets, as it turned out, could have used a hit in any one of those three at-bats, as they were having trouble getting the big hit.

Trailing by 1 run late in the game, the Mets were able to tie the D-Backs 3–3 in the bottom the eighth inning, when Roger Cedeño hit a sacrifice fly to score Edgardo Alfonzo. The Mets were having a hard time getting all that much going offensively, however, leaving 10 runners on base and going just 1-for-8 with runners in scoring position. Pratt himself was responsible for 0-for-4 of that statistic.

With the game tied 3–3 in the bottom of the eighth inning, Arizona manager Buck Showalter went to his closer, Matt Mantei, who was acquired from the Florida Marlins on July 8. Between the two teams, Mantei had earned a total of 32 saves during the regular season, and he was now standing in the middle of the diamond at Shea Stadium in a tie ballgame.

Todd Pratt pumps his fist as he rounds the bases and heads for home after homering off of Matt Mantei.

Mantei retired the first man to face him in the 10th inning, Robin Ventura, who sent a fly ball to right field. The next man to face Mantei was the struggling backup catcher, Todd Pratt. The last thing on the minds of just about every single one of the 56,177 fans, the players and coaches in the dugouts and bullpens, and anyone else who happened to be on hand, was a walk-off, game-winning home run from Pratt.

Chris Berman had the call on ESPN:

Oh, that one's hit well to center field. Finley goes back, back, back—it's *over*, it's *over!*—Todd Pratt, one of the most unlikely of heroes!

Mets announcer Gary Cohen had the honors on WFAN radio:

Fly ball deep to center field, back goes Finley, going back, warning track, at the wall, jumping—and—it's *outta here*, it's *outta here!* Pratt hit it over the fence. Finley jumped, and he missed it. The Mets win the ballgame. The Mets win the ballgame.

Each announcer, like everyone else at Shea Stadium, paused for just a moment, as it appeared as if Finley had made the catch. Even Pratt stopped between first and second base, thinking the Gold Glover may have come down with the ball. The entire stadium fell completely quiet.

"I thought he caught it at first," Mantei told reporters after the game. "But then I saw him bang up against the wall, so I knew it was over. . . . I threw a fastball right down the middle of the plate. I think it was the first hit [Pratt] got in the series. What a great time for it."

"When he hit it, I saw Steve Finley going back real slowly," Mets reserve outfielder Shawon Dunston told reporters after the game. "He timed it. He's not a Gold Glover for nothing. When he came down calm, I thought he had it. Then he came down too calm, and I knew it was gone."

Even Finley felt that he should have made the play.

"I felt like I should have caught it. It hit the end of my glove. I've caught a lot of those before," Finley said after the game.

Not that one though. And in an instant, Shea Stadium went from silence to utter pandemonium that shook the building.

Seventeen years after the blast, Pratt remained humble about his role in 1999 and what it meant to him.

"It didn't change my life. Not at all," Pratt told the *Albany Times Union* in 2016. "Maybe it gave me a few more years in the big leagues. . . . I just appreciate having the opportunity."

The home run was the biggest highlight in the career of Pratt, who—humble or not—on that October day in 1999 forever inscribed his name in the *Book of Mets*.

"That was his shining moment, to be sure," said Mets broadcaster Howie Rose.

26

The Grand Slam Single (1999)

There are certain players throughout team history that have become so associated with a specific moment that all you need to do is say their name and the immediate response is that moment. For example, if you say "Endy Chavez" to a Mets fan, he or she immediately thinks of Endy's leaping grab in the 2006 NLCS. If you say "Tug McGraw," fans immediately think of "Ya Gotta Believe!" And if you say "Robin Ventura," fans immediately think of the Grand Slam Single.

Ventura was a star by the time he arrived in New York prior to the 1999 season, having played 10 seasons with the Chicago White Sox and winning five Gold Glove Awards at third base. He didn't disappoint in his first year with the Mets, batting .301 with 32 home runs and a career-high 120 runs batted in. Along the way, Ventura won his sixth Gold Glove and quickly became a fan favorite. Not known as a home run hitter, he also had a knack for coming up big with the bases loaded. For his career, 18 of his 294 home runs were grand slams. In 1999 alone, Ventura had 3 slams for the Mets.

By the time the 1999 National League Championship Series rolled around, it seemed as though the Mets had been through multiple postseasons. They had defeated the Reds in the one-game tiebreaker to officially reach the playoffs, thanks to the brilliance of Al Leiter, and had pushed aside the Arizona Diamondbacks, thanks to the timely heroics of Todd Pratt. Now, it was on to the hated Atlanta Braves.

The Braves were no strangers to this spot, as in 1999 they were playing in their eighth-straight NLCS. The Mets had not appeared in this series since 1988. In September, it seemed unlikely that the division rivals would meet after the regular season. The Braves had taken nine of 12 games against the Mets and late in the season, assuming the Mets were dead and buried, had verbally taken on their fans.

Following the Mets' 11-inning loss to the Braves on September 30, Atlanta third baseman Chipper Jones was quoted as saying, "Now all the Mets fans can go home and put on their Yankees stuff." Braves closer John Rocker said, "How many times do we have to beat them before their fans will shut up?"

However, the Mets came back from the dead and made it all the way to face the Braves in the NLCS, where they appeared overmatched early on. The Braves won Game One behind a strong performance by Greg Maddux and Game Two behind strong pitching from Kevin Millwood. For Game Three, the NLCS shifted to Shea Stadium, where Mets fans were ready. However, the Mets' bats were not, and Atlanta came away with the slimmest of 1–0 victories. The Mets were now down 3–0 and seemed to be heading for their second death of the season. No team had ever come back from a 3–0 deficit to win a playoff series.

In Game Four, the Mets played tough but were trailing 2–1 in the bottom of the eighth inning. It was at that point that John Olerud came up against Rocker with runners on first and second. The baserunners—Roger Cedeño and Melvin Mora—promptly took off and succeeded on a double steal, putting the tying run on third and moving the potential winning run to second. After the game, Mora said, he had decided the Mets should double-steal as soon as he saw Rocker come in.

"I ran to second when Rocker came in," Mora told reporters. "I told [Roger] let's steal. We've got to play the game like that. He said, 'I don't want to get thrown out.' I told him not to worry about that."

Braves manager Bobby Cox acknowledged after the game that his team was expecting the double swipe. Their plan was to ignore the speedy Cedeño heading to third and try to gun down Mora at second. That plan was relayed to his catcher Eddie Pérez.

"That was the plan; everybody understood it," Cox said. "We just couldn't do it. We might throw him out on a fastball, but it was a slow curve, and it was too low. He can't throw all fastballs there. He's got to mix them up. If they guess right, they guess right. You can't do anything about it. Eddie had to reach for the ball way down here. It was down and way out. It wasn't good."

For Rocker's part, keeping the runners close was hardly an option. His one goal was to get Olerud out.

"I got a terrible pickoff move," Rocker told reporters after the game. "What am I going to do? I'm not going to keep them from running. My pickoff move is awful. I had every intention of getting Olerud out."

Olerud now had two runners in scoring position and did what he did best—grounded a single up the middle, just out of the reach of shortstop Ozzie Guillén. Both runners scored, and the Mets had a 3–2 lead.

"That's one of the cheaper hits I've given up in my entire life," Rocker said when asked about what would end up being the game-winning hit. "It's not like it was a double off the wall. It was just a well-placed three-hop groundball."

In any event, Armando Benítez retired the Braves in the top of the ninth, and the Mets were clinging to life in the series, down 3–1.

By the time Game Five rolled around, many of the Mets veterans were hurting. Injuries had taken a toll on players such as Piazza and Ventura—who was 0-for-12 at the plate in the NLCS. However, both were in the starting lineup for the crucial contest. The Mets, thanks to Olerud—the Game Four hero—took an early 2–0 lead after a first-inning, 2-run homer. However, the Braves tied the game in the top of the fourth inning. That was all the scoring in the game for what seemed like an eternity. As a steady rain pelted the players and fans at Shea, the Mets and Braves exchanged jabs for the next 10 innings over what seemed like 10 hours.

Then, in the top of the 15th inning, the Braves seemed to put the Mets away for good when Walt Weiss singled and a run-scoring triple by Keith Lockhart followed. The Braves were three outs away from the World Series, and the Mets were three outs away from the offseason. But then again, if that happened, you wouldn't be reading about this game in a book called *Miracle Moments in New York Mets History*!

"After the Braves went one up in the 15th, every guy in the dugout kept saying, 'We're going to do this,'" Mets manager Bobby Valentine told reporters after the game. "I must have heard it 15 times."

In the bottom of the 15th inning, Shawon Dunston led off against Atlanta's Kevin McGlinchy with a single to center. The next batter was Matt Franco, who walked. After Edgardo Alfonzo bunted the runners over to second and third,

Part Two

Olerud was walked to load the bases. Todd Pratt—who had replaced a hurting Piazza in the 14th inning and played the role of hero in the National League Division Series—then walked with the bases loaded to force in the tying run. The next man to come to the plate—with the winning run 90 feet away—was Ventura, who was 1-for-18 in the NLCS.

"It's different when the bases are loaded and the guy has already walked a guy," Ventura told reporters after the game. "He can't really fool around and throw a bunch of pitches in the dirt. So I'm just trying to get a ball in the air so the guy can score."

At 9:46 p.m., five hours and 46 minutes after the game started, McGlinchy delivered a 2–1 pitch to Ventura. This was how it sounded from Gary Cohen on WFAN:

> The 2–1 pitch—a drive in the air to deep right field, that ball headed toward the wall, that ball is—*outta here, outta here*—a game-winning grand slam home run off the bat of Robin Ventura!

As Ventura round first base, however, Pratt—who had touched second base and turned around to charge toward Ventura—lifted his teammate into the air with a giant bear hug as he tried to advance to second base. The game was over the instant the runner from third touched home. The Mets had won. All of his teammates joined Pratt and mobbed Ventura, who was stuck between first and second. The Mets had somehow advanced to Game Six on the strangest of "home runs." The scoreboard immediately changed to Mets 7, Braves 3. However, right after the play, official scorer Red Foley changed the ruling to a single, and the final score would officially be 4–3. It really didn't make a difference; it was a victory, and the Mets had lived to play another day.

"I saw it go over, and then I just ran to first," Ventura told reporters after the game. "I saw Todd Pratt running back at me. As long as I touched first, we won. So that's fine with me. It just seems like this team responds to dire situations. We just play another day. It seems like we've been saying that for about a month and a half now. We can't lose another game. We're happy to just be playing."

As it turns out, Pratt did not intentionally prevent Ventura's grand slam because the fact was, at the time, Pratt had no idea the ball went over the fence.

"I saw the trajectory, and I thought it was a gapper," Pratt explained to reporters the day after the game. "I knew I had to touch second, and the game was over. And then I used the base as a sprinter's block, and I ran to Robin."

Mets manager Bobby Valentine and his team mob Robin Ventura after he launched his
"Grand Slam Single."

It wasn't the first time in baseball history that a home run, in the end, wasn't a home run. In 1929, Frank Sigafoos of the Detroit Tigers launched the first home run of his career against the St. Louis Browns. However, before the homer was hit, the home plate umpire had called a balk on the Browns pitcher, meaning the ball was dead. Unfortunately for Sigafoos, that would be the only home run he would ever hit—or not hit.

In 1978, Baltimore's John Lowenstein ripped a home run off California pitcher Paul Hartzell. The only thing is, umpire Bill Deegan had called time just before Hartzell delivered the pitch because a paper airplane came sailing down from the stands and onto the field.

For Mets fans, all other would-be homers fall short of Ventura's. While things didn't end well for the Mets in Game Six of the 1999 NLCS, Game Five will be talked about forever. That was the night that Robin Ventura hit the grand slam that never was. Well, at first it was, but then it wasn't. What it is, however, is the most talked-about non–home run in team history.

27

Benny Goes Boom (2000)

And like that, he's gone.

Few players come from nowhere and fade into obscurity as quickly as Benny Agbayani did. After being drafted by the Mets in 1993, Agbayani—a bulky player with a huge smile—spent the next six seasons moving up through the minors. Finally, in 1998 he got his first taste of the majors and made the team as spring training broke in 1999. That first full season, Agbayani hit 14 home runs for the Mets—11 in the first half—and played all three outfield positions. He proved to be a dependable utility player and someone who could provide pop off the bench.

Before the 2000 season, a lot of things were up in the air for Agbayani, who was not assured of making the team and had even requested a trade. But by the opener, Agbayani was penciled in as the starting left fielder for the Mets and paid immediate dividends. After an Opening Day loss to the Chicago Cubs in Tokyo—the first of a two-game season-opening series in Japan—the Mets needed a spark to ensure that they did not travel nearly seven thousand miles for nothing. That spark came from Agbayani, who, in the top of the 11th inning of a 1–1 game, launched a grand slam to dead center to give the Mets a 5–1 victory. Still, Agbayani's future with the team was uncertain.

"I'm glad he's here today," Mets manager Bobby Valentine told reporters after the win. "I'm glad he was here last year, helping us win games. I think he's a good player."

Agbayani ended up having a very solid season for the Mets, appearing in 119 games for the team, swatting a career-high 15 home runs, and driving home 68 runs. He was also a fan favorite. Never was that clearer than in the 2000 National League Division Series against the San Francisco Giants.

Benny Agbayani watches the flight of his game-winning home run.

Part Two

Benny Agbayani celebrates after homering against the San Francisco Giants in the 2000 NLDS.

After getting a hit in each of the first two games of the series, Agbayani, and the Mets, entered Game Three with the series tied one game apiece. Game Three was a critical tipping point for the best-of-five NLDS.

It seemed unlikely as Game Three moved along that Agbayani would be a hero, as he had gone 0-for-5 through the first 12 innings. The Mets and Giants were deadlocked in a classic matchup where neither offense seemed willing or able to get the big hit. The Mets had tied the game 2–2 in the bottom of the eighth inning on Edgardo Alfonzo's run-scoring double. Neither team was able to score in the ninth, 10th, 11th, or 12th innings.

In the top of the 13th inning, the Giants were able to get two runners on, but Mets pitcher Rick White got Barry Bonds to pop out to end the inning.

In the bottom of the 13th, Robin Ventura led off the inning against Aaron Fultz with a groundout to second base. The next batter was Agbayani, and Joe Buck had the call on FOX-TV:

Agbayani hits it deep left center—13th inning—Mets win Game Three!

"Bobby Valentine told me things have a way of working out," Agbayani told reporters after the game. "I didn't understand that. Now I do."

As it turned out, Agbayani was only the biggest clutch player of the Mets' playoff run in 2000 for 24 hours. By the following night, there was a new hero. However, for that one night, Benny Agbayani owned Shea Stadium, and he owned New York.

28

Jones's Shutout (2000)

Throughout baseball history, there have been many men who happened to share the same name. The Mets alone have had eight such combos. Of course, Mets fans remember *the* Pedro Martinez, who pitched for the Blue and Orange from 2005 through 2008. During his career, Martinez won the Cy Young Award three times, was an eight-time All-Star, and was elected to the Hall of Fame in 2015. The "other" Pedro Martinez—also a pitcher—had a five-year career from 1993 through 1997, including five games with the Mets in 1996. This Pedro Martinez won a total of seven games during his career—212 fewer games than the man with whom he shared his name. However, that is just the most recent of Mets same-name guys.

Two of the Mets' same-name duos need a bit of an explanation and perhaps even an asterisk. Firstly, one pair is a father and a son—as Sandy Alomar Sr. played for the Mets in 1967 and Sandy Alomar Jr. played the last eight games of his 20-year career for New York in 2007. The other asterisk goes to Shawn Green, who played for the Mets in 2006 and 2007, and Sean Green, who played in Flushing from 2009 through 2010.

The others are all legit, and they include Bob Johnson (second baseman in 1967) and Bob Johnson (pitcher in 1969), Mike Marshall (pitcher in 1981) and Mike Marshall (first baseman in 1990), and Chris Young (pitcher in 2011 and 2012) and Chris Young (left fielder in 2014).

What is most interesting, however, are the same-name guys who actually played for the Mets during the same season. That has happened twice. The first time this occurred for the Mets was in 1962 when they had two pitchers named Bob Miller. The first one (or second one) was a twenty-three-year-old right-handed starter whom the Mets had acquired from the St. Louis Cardinals. He had a 1–12 record for the Mets in 1962. The other Mets pitcher named Bob Miller, a lefty, appeared in only 17 games for the Mets—all in relief—and had a record of 2–2.

The Mets announced in May how they would tell the two Bob Millers apart.

"R. L. Miller is Robert Lane Miller, the right-hander," Mets Publicity Director Tom Meany told reporters. "R. G. Miller is Robert Gerald Miller, the left-hander we got from Cincinnati. R. L. wears number 24, and R. G. will wear number 23."

Meany continued, explaining that the two men would most likely room together on the road, having some fun with the press—and the situation.

"That way," he said, "when somebody telephones Bob Miller they have a 50-50 chance of getting the right one."

In October of 1962, when R. G. Miller was released by the Mets, in its reporting of the story, the *New York Times* stated, "The release of Miller leaves the Mets with only one pitcher named Bob Miller."

Three decades later, the Mets found themselves in a similar situation. In 1991, the Mets used their second first-round pick—the 36th overall—to select a right-handed pitcher named Bobby Jones out of Cal State University, Fresno. By 1993, Jones had made it to the Mets and had his best year with the team in 1997, when he went 15–9 and was named to the National League All-Star team. Jones struggled a bit with performance and injuries in 1998 and 1999 and by early 2000 it looked as though his days with the Mets might be numbered.

Coincidentally, prior to the start of the 2000 season, the Mets had fortified their pitching staff by making a trade with the Colorado Rockies. The pitcher the Mets received was—of course—Bobby Jones. This Bobby Jones was a lefty, however. Despite spending most of the season with the Norfolk Tides of the International League, where he made 22 starts, Jones was up in the majors with the Mets for 11 games. The left-handed Bobby Jones actually grew up in New Jersey rooting for the Mets and made his first major-league start against the Mets at Shea in 1998. During the time that the two Joneses were on the Mets' roster at the same time, they were distinguished on paper as Bobby J. Jones and Bobby M. Jones.

Heading into the 2000 season, it was unclear how much the right-handed Bobby Jones was going to be able to give the Mets. He had suffered shoulder problems for much of the 1999 season, causing him to miss three months of the season. As the 2000 campaign began, Jones's troubles continued, and by early June, the Mets had seen enough and decided to send him down to triple-A Norfolk to try to get back on track. Jones had enough major-league service that he did not have to accept the demotion; however, he decided to do what the Mets had asked.

"You pitch in the major leagues for seven seasons, and all of a sudden things go bad for you," Jones told reporters. "There's been a lot of restless times and a lot of sleepless nights trying to figure out exactly what's going on. But sometimes you have to swallow your pride and figure out what's best."

Just to add a little extra depth to the situation—and this chapter—when Jones was sent down to Norfolk, the Mets recalled—of course—the other Bobby Jones.

After spending a week tinkering with his delivery in the minors, Jones was recalled to the Mets—and yes, the other Bobby Jones was sent back down to Norfolk. Following a strong eight-inning performance in his first game back in the majors, the right-hander was optimistic that his time in the minors was time well spent.

"You have an opportunity to work on things without having that much pressure on you," Jones told reporters. "I think that I needed that, to go down there and just be able to work on things."

The biggest start of Jones's career, however, would be three-and-a-half months later, when the Mets tapped him to start Game Four—the potential clincher—against the San Francisco Giants in the National League Division Series. Jones pitched the best game of his life, retiring the Giants in order in eight of the nine innings he pitched. The only man to reach base with a hit was Jeff Kent, who doubled in the top of the fifth inning. Other than that, two walks was all that Jones allowed. The victory lifted the Mets to the National League Championship Series and lifted Jones from the pain of a mid-season minor-league demotion to the euphoria of postseason immortality.

"I felt good from when I got up this morning, and I just wanted to come out and have a good game and give my team a chance to win," Jones told CNNSI on the field after the game. "I was just fortunate enough to have my great stuff tonight. I was able to change speeds and had some great plays made behind me."

Bobby Jones pitched the game of a lifetime against the Giants, capping it by getting Barry Bonds to fly out to center field.

Mets fans listening on WFAN heard the call of the final out from Bob Murphy:

> The pitch on the way to Bonds, fly ball hit to center, can he run it down, on the run Payton—*makes the catch*—it's all over, the Mets win it!

Following the last out of the game, Jones was mobbed by his teammates in a throng that bounced up and down for minutes between the pitcher's mound and third base. Murphy's excitement was evident:

> They're all racing to the mound and mobbing Bobby Jones. What a magnificent game! The Mets have never had a better ballgame pitched in their 39-year history!

For Jones's part, following the final out, things were a bit surreal.

"I really didn't know what to do," he told reporters. "I had never been in that situation before."

29

One Throw, Two Outs (2006)

One of the greatest things about watching baseball is that on any given day or night you may witness something that you have never seen before. Perhaps you will see an infield turn a triple play, a batter hit for the cycle, or even a pitcher toss a no-hitter or perfect game. While each of these accomplishments is extremely rare in baseball, it is not unthinkable to believe that any one of them can be accomplished.

However, there are some things that you witness during a game that simply boggle the mind to the point where you wonder if it will ever happen again. One such moment took place during Game One of the 2006 National League Divisional Playoff Series between the Mets and Los Angeles Dodgers. It was an afternoon game at Shea Stadium with 56,979 fans looking on.

In the top of the second inning with the Dodgers batting against the Mets' John Maine, second baseman Jeff Kent—a former Met—led off with a line-drive single to center field. The next better was J. D. Drew, who reached on an infield single, putting runners on first and second with nobody out.

The next batter was Russell Martin, who rifled a line drive to right field. Shawn Green—a former Dodger—played the carom off the wall perfectly and fired to the cutoff man José Valentín—a former Dodger—who made the absolute perfect relay throw to catcher Paul Lo Duca—yes, also a former Dodger. Announcer Gary Thorne was handling the national broadcast for ESPN:

That's going to bounce off the wall, late start for Kent, they got a shot at the plate, here's the relay, Valentín in time? He's out! Second runner, he's out! He got 'em both! Kent is out, Drew is out—at the plate!

The late start by Kent that Thorne mentioned live was the cause for the traffic jam at the plate. Drew, who took off from first when Martin made contact, nearly caught up to Kent as the two men reached third base.

"As I went to throw my hands up [to stop Kent], out of the corner of my eye, here comes J. D.," Dodgers third-base coach Rich Donnelly told reporters after the game. "If I hold Jeff, we've got two guys on third."

For his part, Drew never gave Kent a second thought.

"I thought the play was going to be on me at home plate," Drew said after the game. "I thought Jeff would score standing up."

Out in right field, Green didn't know or care what the runners were thinking; he was just doing the best he could to start the play.

"When you get a ball like that, you are very well trained as an outfielder that you get to the ball as fast as you can and try to grab it and release it with a strong throw to the relay man, and that's what I did," said Green, who was acquired

Catcher Paul Lo Duca tags out J. D. Drew at the plate.

by the Mets late in the 2006 season. "You start your throwing motion really before you even see the relay man, so as I was winding up I picked up Valentín and adjusted mid-motion and got him the ball, and he did the rest to get it to Lo Duca."

After starting the play, Green vividly remembers the rest.

"Once Valentín got the ball, I could see the play unfolding, and like everyone in the stadium and watching on TV, after he made the first tag you just wanted to scream, 'Look behind you, look behind you.' Sure enough, he saw it just in the nick of time and turned an incredible double play. You don't see that very often."

Although he was new to the Mets, Green had played in Shea Stadium's right field plenty of times as a visitor and knew what to expect in terms of how the ball might ricochet.

"You get to know the fields pretty well and take balls and learn the bounces," Green said. "I was definitely trying to time it and place myself in the best possible position, and fortunately it worked out that day."

It wasn't lost on Green that all of the players involved in that play for the Mets were former Dodgers.

"Of course, anytime you're playing against a team that you had recently played for there's extra icing on the cake when you're able to contribute to a victory for your new team and beat the team that either traded you or passed on your services," Green said. "And that was the case for all three of us involved in that play. You always want to beat your former team."

The Mets went on to win that game and the next two in their sweep of Los Angeles, enabling them to advance to the 2006 National League Championship Series.

30

"He Made the Catch!" (2006)

In April of 1996, the Mets signed a seventeen-year-old outfielder from Valencia, Venezuela, named Endy Chavez. Ten years and five months later, he would make the most incredible catch in the history of the franchise. However, it was far from a straight line from *A* to *B* for Chavez—or the Mets.

After moving around the Mets farm system for three seasons, Chavez never reached anything above high-A ball. While the Mets were making their way to the 2000 World Series, a young Chavez batted .298 for St. Lucie of the Florida State League with 20 doubles and 38 steals. However, following the season, Chavez was claimed by the Kansas City Royals in the Rule 5 Draft. That started a series of transactions for Chavez that are a challenge to follow.

Three months after being claimed by Kansas City, Chavez became a part of a bizarre sequence of events between the Mets and Royals. On March 30, 2001, the Royals returned Chavez to the Mets. Later that same day, the Mets traded Chavez back to the Royals. Imagine the paperwork. Things continued to be weird for Chavez, as the following December, he was selected off waivers by the Detroit Tigers from the Royals. Two months later, he was selected off waivers by the Mets from the Tigers. Three weeks after that, he was selected off waivers by the Montreal Expos from the Mets. Everyone—and no one—seemed to know what to do with Endy Chavez.

In December of 2005, Chavez—now a member of the Washington Nationals after Montreal relocated—was traded to the Philadelphia Phillies for veteran

Marlon Byrd. However, after one season playing with the Phillies, Chavez was granted free agency. Finally, the direct line to an incredible, once-in-a-lifetime catch was in place. One day after being granted free agency once again, Chavez signed with the Mets.

Heading into the 2006 season, the Mets had a solid starting outfield, consisting of Cliff Floyd in left, Carlos Beltrán in center, and Xavier Nady in right. Among the outfield reserve players was twenty-one-year-old top prospect Lastings Milledge. However, as it turned out, it was Chavez who would play in 133 games for the Mets in 2006, more than any outfielder other than Beltrán. Chavez's time was split nearly equally in left, center, and right field.

On August 22, 2006, the Mets acquired veteran right fielder Shawn Green from the Arizona Diamondbacks. The surplus of outfielders did not seem to hurt Chavez, who quickly earned the respect of Green.

"[Endy] was up there with a lot of great outfielders," said Green, who spent 15 years as an outfielder in the majors and was a two-time All-Star and a Gold Glove winner. "I think defensively he was one of the best, including guys who won a bunch of Gold Gloves."

While Chavez's glove was always one of his strongest attributes, in 2006 he had one of his best seasons offensively, batting .306 with 22 doubles. He was a key role player as the Mets coasted to their first National League East division crown in 18 years. Though young stars such as David Wright and José Reyes and veterans such as Beltrán and Carlos Delgado led the team, Chavez filled an important role.

Chavez went on to play in each of the Mets' playoff games that year, batting .375 in the three-game sweep of the Los Angeles Dodgers in the National League Division Series. However, it was during the final playoff game he would ever play for the Mets that Chavez would leave his everlasting mark.

The 2006 National League Division Series was a back-and-forth affair, with the Mets and St. Louis Cardinals alternating wins to a 3–3 series tie. Game Seven would decide who would advance to the World Series. With the game tied 1–1, the Cardinals had one man on and one out at the top of the sixth inning as Scott Rolen stepped up to the plate.

What happened next would live on as one of the greatest highlights in Mets history. Shawn Green does not need to see the replays, though, as he saw everything unfold from where he stood in right field.

Part Two

It started when Rolen sent a fly ball to deep left field.

"I knew [Endy] would give it a good shot, but it just didn't seem like there was going to be enough room for him to pull it in," Green remembered. "The only hope I had was that at that time of year the air is pretty heavy and it had cooled off quite a bit and you know as an outfielder if the balls are just not carrying. Off the bat, it seemed like it was going to be even farther over the fence than it was. But fortunately it didn't carry, and Endy got up there really high and timed it perfectly, and somehow the ball didn't snap out of his glove when it coiled backwards."

Mets television announcer Gary Cohen was doing an inning of radio for WFAN:

Endy Chavez leaped high into the night to snag Scott Rolen's deep fly.

Fastball hit in the air to left field, that's deep, back goes Chavez, back near the wall, leaping, and—*he made the catch!*—he took a home run away from Rolen!

Even FOX television announcer Joe Buck, who often does not let emotion enter his calls, was energized by the Chavez play, capping the call with a signature remark often used by his father, Hall of Fame announcer Jack Buck:

Scott Rolen hits one into deep left field, back at the wall, a leap—and a *catch!* Endy Chavez takes a home run away and turns it into a double play. Unbelievable!

"It was amazing," Green said. "I'm sure it was the best catch that I have ever seen."

Sports columnist Ian O'Connor described the play as only he could.

"Chavez made his Bob Beamon leap into a forever corner of sports legend, going high over the left field wall to rob Scott Rolen of a sure two-run homer," O'Connor wrote in *The Journal News* in White Plains, New York.

The catch—which became the first out of an inning-ending double play when the Mets doubled-off Jim Edmonds trying to get back to first—could have been a dramatic springboard to victory.

"At that point, I really thought we were going to win the game," Green said. "It was a nice momentum swing, but unfortunately it didn't quite get us to that next step."

Unfortunately for the Mets, the Cardinals would hit another blast to left field in the top of the ninth—this one by Yadier Molina, and this one out of the reach of Chavez—a two-run homer. Sportswriter Lee Jenkins of the *New York Times* summed it up best: "On the first fly ball, Chavez had a play," Jenkins wrote. "On the second one, he only had a view."

Despite a rally in the bottom of the ninth in which the Mets loaded the bases, the Blue and Orange fell short. Mets fans remember the ending all too well: Beltrán struck out looking—something for which he has taken a lot of abuse over the years—and the Mets' season was suddenly over.

Two years later, Chavez's career with the Mets was also over. After two very steady seasons as a fourth outfielder patrolling the expansive Shea territory, Chavez was part of a three-team, 12-player trade. When the dust cleared, Chavez was a member of the Seattle Mariners in a deal that sent reliever J. J. Putz to the Mets. Yet Chavez was not in Seattle for long. The fact is, he never was any one place very long. The long and winding road of Endy Chavez transactions continued throughout his career. Over the next nine seasons, Chavez played for the Texas Rangers, Baltimore Orioles, Mariners (again), Bridgeport Bluefish of the Atlantic League, and—most recently—the Pericos de Puebla of the Mexican Baseball League in 2017.

More than 10 years after robbing Scott Rolen at Shea Stadium on that October night, Chavez was playing center field for the Navegantes del Magallanes of the Venezuelan Winter League. Now thirty-eight years old, Chavez brought everyone back in time when José Osuna sent a long fly ball to center. The ball, much like Rolen's a decade earlier, seemed destined to be a home run. However, much like 2006's long fly, this one too ended up in the webbing of Chavez's mitt. Endy leaped into the air, caught the ball—which was over the home-run line, although not as much as Rolen's was—and calmly landed on his feet. He flipped the ball out of his glove and threw it back into the infield as if to say, "Been there, done that." Clearly, Chavez never lost his skills—or his flair for the dramatic.

In many ways, and to many Mets fans, the Chavez play is a hard one to reconcile. While the play itself is clearly incredible, it ended up being a memory of a pennant that could have been. Still, despite the bittersweet memories of the play, Shawn Green summed up Endy Chavez's catch best: "It was spectacular," he said.

31

The 2015 Run

The Mets' magical run to the 2015 World Series is complicated—and all fans know it.

At the start of the 2015 season, the Mets were not exactly presenting the most impressive of lineups. Sure, they had plenty of young arms, but coming off six-straight sub-.500 seasons, the Mets had injury issues and various players going in and out of their starting lineup. By mid-June, things started to really get painful. After losing the first seven of an eight-game road trip, the Mets dropped to 36–37 but still somehow found themselves only 3½ games behind first-place Washington.

"I remember the stretch where they had lost seven straight games and scored a total of 9 runs," said SNY field reporter Steve Gelbs. "The offense had just been completely nonexistent for the first half of the season. The thing was, the Nationals weren't running away with it, so there was always this lingering belief that if the Mets could hang in there and stay close enough that the front office might be willing to take a fling and go for it."

One month later, as the trade deadline approached, the Mets made a deal with the Atlanta Braves that helped solidify the team they would become for the rest of the season. The Mets sent two minor leaguers to Atlanta and in return received veterans Juan Uribe and Kelly Johnson. One week later, the Mets traded for Carlos Gomez, but then they didn't, and instead ended up with a pretty good hitter named Yoenis Céspedes (see Chapter 16).

Daniel Murphy and Jeurys Familia celebrate after the Mets won the 2015 National League pennant.

"That night when they made the trade that never was for Carlos Gomez—in that moment, when we thought that the trade was going to be made—it made total sense," Gelbs said. "We expected it. Now what happened the next couple of days was kind of surreal. We had heard a lot about [Jay] Bruce for [Zack] Wheeler, and that didn't happen, and at the last minute the trade is made for Céspedes. At the moment you think, *OK, they are going for it; it's not the guy they originally wanted, but they are going for it, and it's going to energize the team.*"

Energize the team, it did! The Mets went on to have a September to remember and cruised to the National League East title and a date with the Los Angeles Dodgers in the National League Division Series.

"It felt like every night something special was going to happen, it really did—especially when Céspedes really started going on his rampage," Gelbs said. "Once he hit his groove, it felt like he was hitting a monstrous home run in a big spot every night. Then it became a kind of a train where the momentum never stopped. It was every single night, and it felt like they couldn't lose."

This is where things started to get complicated—and that is because of who the Mets hero ended up being for the next two weeks.

Prior to the 2010 season, it looked as though Daniel Murphy's career with the Mets was in serious jeopardy. After hurting his knee in spring training, he was replaced in the lineup by a slick-fielding player by the name of Ike Davis. Then, while playing in a rehab assignment at triple-A Buffalo, Murphy suffered a serious injury and missed the rest of the season. While he did come back in 2011, and was batting .320 into August, he suffered a season-ending injury once again after colliding with Atlanta's José Constanza. Murphy, it seemed, was snakebitten.

In 2012, a healthy Murphy was moved from first base to second base and was a constant in the Mets lineup in 2013 and an All-Star in 2014. In 2015, Murphy's last year under contract with the Mets, he split his time playing second base and third base and batted .281, his lowest average since his rookie year. Not at all known as a significant power threat, Murphy did swat a career-high 14 home runs in 2015. That season was also highlighted by some terrific defensive plays from Murphy, who at second base often exhibited the flair for the dramatic but struggled on simpler plays. One thing was for sure—he also played with a lot of heart and a lot of spirit.

In the 2015 National League Division Series against the Los Angeles Dodgers, Murphy played like a man on a mission, batting .333 with 3 home runs and 5 runs batted in. Those 3 homers came in consecutive games for Murphy and the Mets, with his first home run of the series in Game Three and his second in Game Four. His final homer of the series was a game-winning blast in Game Five, which sent the Mets to the National League Championship Series—and one step closer to the World Series.

"I got the heater finally in the spot that I was looking for," Murphy told reporters after the game, "and fortunately I didn't miss it."

However, Murphy did not stop there. He went on to personally dismantle the Chicago Cubs pitching staff in the National League Championship Series, as he went 9-for-17—a .529 batting average—with 4 more home runs and 6 RBIs. Murphy's offensive heroics, combined with shutdown pitching by Matt Harvey, Noah Syndergaard, Jacob deGrom, Bartolo Colón, and Jeurys Familia, propelled the Mets to a four-game sweep of the Cubs and the team's first National League Pennant since 2000. Howie Rose, the Mets radio voice on WOR-710, was more than happy to supply the word picture:

Here's the payoff pitch from Familia to Fowler—on the way—and it's in there, strike three called! The Mets win the pennant! The New York Mets have won the National League pennant!

"When Familia struck out Dexter Fowler to win the pennant and those words came out of my mouth—'the Mets win the pennant'—that was my top moment," Rose said. "Hopefully there's going to be one that is better than that at some time down the road. Those words 'the Mets win the pennant' made it very difficult for me to continue without choking up. It meant that much. My mind flashed back to every game I had ever played in the schoolyard and was making believe that I was an announcer and every game I was ever at rooting for the Mets, and it really all just circled back over the entirety of the Mets' existence and my history with them."

How the Mets came together as a team in 2015 was truly remarkable. They were able to blend veteran players, young players, new players and go on a magical run that took them deep in October.

"They really had every single aspect of a winning team, and it was a dream run," Gelbs said. "No one really was expecting it, but it was a heck of ride to witness and be a part of."

So here is the complicated part—everyone knows that the Mets wouldn't have won the 2015 National League pennant without the outstanding play of Murphy, including his seven-straight postseason games with a home run.

"It was ridiculous," Gelbs said. "It was baffling to watch. For all of the great pitching and everything else, when you look at that run, Daniel Murphy was the catalyst behind that run."

However, Murphy now holds a very different place in the hearts and minds of Mets fans, now playing for the team's most hated rival—the Washington Nationals. The Mets, perhaps thinking that Murphy's postseason success was more of an exception than the rule, chose not to re-sign the second baseman who, in turn, signed in Washington.

"In retrospect, he had completely changed himself as a player, and we were seeing the real Daniel Murphy. But in the moment it appeared to be just this incredible outlier of a hot streak," Gelbs said. "In the moment it was, 'Wow, what a run of a lifetime that came at the most opportune time,' but looking back he had really changed as a player. And all of his hard work had kicked in at that moment, and we were seeing the beginning stages of what is now one of the best, most feared hitters in the league."

In 2016, Murphy batted .347 with 47 doubles, 25 homers, and 104 runs batted in. More importantly for Mets fans, he hit an incredible .413 with 7 home runs, 6 doubles, and 21 runs batted in his 19 games against the Mets. In 2017, he put up very similar numbers against the National League, although his average was down a bit. Against the Mets he batted .354 with 14 runs batted in. Although he now is one of the best hitters in baseball, plays for the hated Nationals, and destroys Mets pitching, Gelbs believes the memories fans have of 2015 should still be fond ones.

"I think [fans] will view that time for what it was and will always love him for that," he said. "The 2016-and-beyond Daniel Murphy—the Mets fan probably has a hard time wrapping his head around."

In retrospect, the 2015 season will fall into a category with which Mets fans are all too familiar—the Endy Chavez catch, the Robin Ventura Grand Slam Single—great moments that are closely followed by a less-than-memorable outcome. However, one thing is abundantly clear—how a season, or a postseason, or a career plays out often does not lessen the impact of the moment itself.

A miracle moment is still a miracle moment. For those who die hard for the Blue and Orange, all 31 of these moments—passed down from generation to generation—help make up the fabric of what it means to be a Mets fan.

Part Two

PART THREE

EXTRA ACCOLADES

32

Cy DeGrom Dominates

The "win." For as long as anyone can remember, it was the way baseball pitchers were judged. To be a 20-game winner was synonymous with pure excellence—reserved for the best of the best to climb atop a pitching mound. Then there have been the handful of pitchers who won 30 or more games in a season—last accomplished by Denny McLain of the Detroit Tigers in 1968. It was always about the "win."

According to Frank Vaccaro's article entitled "Origin of the Modern Pitching Win" on the Society of American Baseball Research website, the "win" statistic was first invented in 1884 by Henry Chadwick, who is often referred to as the "Father of Baseball" when it came to innovation and statistics. Still, it was not until 1888 that won–lost records were published after games. Exactly 130 years later, Jacob deGrom rendered that same "win" statistic to be irrelevant.

To be fair, there were instances prior to 2018 where wins came under some scrutiny. In 2010, Seattle Mariners ace Felix Hernandez won the American League Cy Young Award with a record of 13-12. However, deGrom—who won 15 games for the Mets in 2017—truly revolutionized the pitching position in 2018.

"He is all about craft and when you look at deGrom and you look at his mechanics and his repeatability, he has found this formula that is extremely unique," said Gary Apple, who has been the host of the Mets' pre- and post-game show on SNY since 2014. "He is not about the glory, he is not about the

Getty Images

headlines—he is about what he does and he takes it very seriously. He's a team guy who wants to win, but he also has this incredible work ethic. The win by a starting pitcher has become somewhat irrelevant and he is the shining example of the fact that you cannot judge a starting pitcher by their record."

In a season during which the Mets would win just 77 games, deGrom started 32 in 2018. Still, as the end of the season approached, it was a race to double-digit wins for deGrom, who sat with a 9-9 record in October. His stuff, however, was absolutely spectacular all season, and he owned a minuscule earned run average.

"Jake has the ability to not only throw hard and have really good stuff, but what separates him from everybody really—and what's really the thing that I think is the hardest thing to do in the game—is the ability to locate pitches," said catcher Kevin Plawecki, who spent many games behind the plate when deGrom was on the mound in 2018. "He comes right at hitters with his best stuff and everybody knows that and guys still can't hit him. It's special to watch and it was definitely special to be a part of when I was there catching him."

When the season was over, deGrom's numbers were staggering—at least most of them. His earned run average was a major league-best 1.70 and was the third lowest of any pitcher with 30 starts in a season since that same 1968 season McLain won his 31 games. In addition, deGrom struck out 269 batters and walked only 46. He did not, however, receive any run support from his teammates and struggled to reach the 10-win mark, finishing the season with a record of 10-9. That did not stop him from getting all but one first-place vote in the National League Cy Young race. A new precedent had been set, as never before had a starting pitcher with only 10 wins won the Cy Young Award. The fact was, there had not been too many pitchers who had the type of season deGrom had in 2018.

"I've been fortunate during my career to catch some really talented pitchers, but Jake stands out for me because of his dominance day in and day out," Plawecki said. "Catching him [in 2018] was a lot of fun for me and to have him be in that Cy Young discussion—and then to win it—and feel like a part of it in a sense, was great."

One year later, deGrom ended up being just as dominant—and just as unfortunate when it came to getting offensive support from his teammates. Although at the start of the season, he didn't resemble his 2018 self at all. In fact, he started the season in a very un-deGrom way, going 4-7 with an earned run average of

3.27. The second half of the season, however, was a very different story, as the Mets ace went 7-1 with a microscopic earned run average of 1.44. For the season, he struck out a National League-leading 255 batters, while walking just 44. Once again, deGrom received all but one first-place vote and was named the National League Cy Young Award winner for the second straight season, just the 11th pitcher in major league history to accomplish that feat.

Perhaps the most impressive thing about deGrom during the 2018 and 2019 seasons—and really throughout his entire career—is the way he goes about his business. He is not flashy, does not crave the spotlight, and is not looking to have a superhero moniker placed upon him. He is a baseball player.

"When you talk about deGrom of course you talk about the talent, but he also has a really good head on his shoulders," Apple said. "There are so many components that go into what makes Jake so great and I think a big part of it is his understanding that it's a short window and that you need to take advantage of that and not waste it."

In 2020, a season that will be long remembered for countless reasons, deGrom made a bid for a third straight Cy Young Award with another strong performance—only to fall just short. He did, however, have an extremely solid season—once again receiving little to no run support—excelling with his usual low earned run average and his league-leading strikeout tally.

33

Welcome, Pete Alonso

The All-Star Game has been a backdrop of many exciting moments in Mets history. In 1975, Jon Matlack was the winning pitcher and co-MVP of the game. In 1979, Lee Mazzilli slammed a game-tying pinch-hit homer. In 1984, rookie phenom Dwight Gooden struck out the side in his first inning of action. In 1986, the Mets sent five representatives, all decked out in white cleats no less. In 2015, deGrom topped Gooden's feat, striking out three straight batters on just 10 pitches. In 2019, Pete Alonso carved out his moment in time during the All-Star festivities—and it wasn't even during the game itself.

Five months earlier, it would have been hard to visualize what happened on that July day in Cleveland. There was no certainty, in fact, that Alonso would even start the season with the Mets. If he began the year in the minors, the Mets would retain an extra year of control on Alonso, an option that the team had exercised on many other young players. There were also questions about Alonso's fielding abilities at first base, which were illustrated during a spring training game when he dropped a routine throw across the diamond and then later blasted a mammoth home run. As it turned out, the mammoth home runs would continue and the fielding turned out to be just fine. The Mets decided to allow Alonso to start the season in the big leagues and, perhaps, it was the best decision the franchise has made in years.

Alonso quickly became a bigger than life character, confident but not cocky, bold but not bullish. He was immediately respected by his teammates and his opponents, and was beloved by the fans. His boyish exuberance was infectious, and after a first half of the season when he launched 34 home runs, he was invited to participate for the National League in the Home Run Derby.

"I think the Home Run Derby transcended just baseball fans. What he did, in his first All-Star Game, doesn't happen very often," said Gary Apple, who hosts the Mets pre- and postgame show on SNY. "Guys set baseball records, yes, but the fact that he was doing these monumental things on these big stages was amazing. And no stage seemed to be too big for him. So I think the Home Run Derby was really a seminal moment where you said, 'Oh man, this guy is the real deal and we've got to watch him and he's fun to watch.' I know that was just an exhibition, but I really think that was really big."

Following the Home Run Derby, Alonso had taken baseball by storm—and Mets fans had a true rookie sensation. Alonso returned from the All-Star Game and continued his chase for the single-season home run record for a rookie, which was owned by the Yankees' Aaron Judge, who set the mark of 52 in 2017. Following a slow start to the second half, Alonso once again got red-hot in August, clubbing homer after homer, adding to his new lore.

Finally, on September 27 at Citi Field—the next to last game of the season—Alonso blasted his way into the record books with home run No. 53. It came against the Atlanta Braves when Alonso turned around a 93 mph fastball from Mike Foltynewicz, depositing it straight into the center-field stands. Alonso extended both arms into the air as he touched first base, and the smile on his face as he rounded second could be seen from space. After crossing the plate, he urged the fans to cheer—as if he was celebrating with them. He hugged on-deck batter Robinson Cano and then approached his teammates, who had all poured out of the dugout to congratulate him. He took the time to hug each and every one of them. Then, again, he acknowledged the fans.

"It was great for the Mets and it was great for baseball because anytime you have a player who does something out of the ordinary or rewrites the history books it draws attention from the baseball world and it draws attention from the casual fan who gets on board," Apple said. "It was of course great for the Mets and for Pete, but I also think it was great for the game. Pete embraced not just his quest to set the record and put up great numbers and be a really good player, but I think he also at a very young age embraced the role that came with it and became a team leader as a rookie who was really respected by all of his teammates."

Getty Images

Following the game, Alonso stood at his locker and spoke to a large throng of reporters, very aware of the history of the game he loves to play.

"I think of old-timey guys like Lou Gehrig, Babe Ruth, Barry Bonds," Alonso said. "To think as a rookie I hit more homers than everyone except for one guy, it's nuts. It's crazy."

When the postseason awards were handed out, Alonso concluded his epic rookie campaign by officially being named the National League Rookie of the Year. He became the sixth Mets player to win the award, joining Tom Seaver, Jon Matlack, Darryl Strawberry, Dwight Gooden, and Jacob deGrom.

"Very few times things that guys do become stuff of legend, and the stuff that he did in 2019 became legendary," Apple said.

Part Three

THREE BONUS WALK-OFFS

Hang on . . . you are not quite done—not yet, at least! There are still three walk-off miracle moments to remember. The term *walk-off*—first used in the late 1980s, in a negative manner, in reference to a pitcher who literally walks off the field after a final-inning loss—has become a celebratory term for baseball's most exciting form of victory. Part of the reason the walk-off is so exciting is that it can only take place in a team's own ballpark, in front of the home fans. So before ending this book, the home fans deserve a little something extra—a few walk-offs. The following three dramatic finishes each ended with the Mets rallying for five runs in the bottom of the ninth inning to pull out incredible victories.

The first of the three took place on June 14, 1980, when the Mets were en route to a last-place, 95-loss season. However, no one told that feisty group of players that that was going to be their destiny—at least not yet.

Heading into that June game, three of the Mets' previous seven victories had come in walk-off fashion. That trend, however, appeared unlikely to continue, as the San Francisco Giants led by a score of 6–2 heading into the bottom of the ninth inning. The Mets seemed out of the game from the start, as the Giants had jumped out to a 4–0 lead in the first inning. Additionally, the Giants had held the Mets hitless until the sixth inning. Still, most of the 22,918 fans that had come out to Shea remained in the building for the bottom of the ninth.

What followed in that inning may seem like fiction but is, indeed, part of Mets history: New York rallied to scratch out two runs against San Francisco reliever Greg Minton on run-scoring hits by Lee Mazzilli and Claudell Washington. Giants manager Dave Bristol then turned to Allen Ripley to face Steve Henderson with two outs and two on. Henderson—who had gotten engaged to his girlfriend just hours earlier—had already struck out three times in the game. He had not yet homered in 1980. In fact, he had not homered since July of 1979.

Possibly emboldened by that fact, Ripley appeared to want to send a message to Henderson, as his second pitch buzzed up and in on the Mets outfielder. Henderson darted backward to avoid getting plunked. The pitch, Henderson would later admit, angered him.

"I try to keep my temper," Henderson told reporters following the game. "But when someone does something like that to me, throwing too close, I sort of turn into a monster."

Two pitches later, the "monster" broke loose and launched the ball to the opposite field and over the fence in right field for a game-winning three-run homer. "That was the first homer I hit that year," Henderson told the New York *Daily News* years later. "I picked the right time."

The fourth walk-off victory in the Mets' last eight wins had everyone in Flushing buzzing.

"It's really revving people up," Mets manager Joe Torre told reporters after the game. "Nobody left the park, even when they're down by six runs. Things just developed, the way they've been developing lately. And when Stevie went up to hit, I knew he was a little tight after striking out those three times. So I just told him to go up and take a swing." And take a swing, he did.

By 1981, Henderson was gone, traded for Dave Kingman—a player who would certainly hit his share of homers in Queens. For that one night in 1980, however, Henderson had his very own miraculous Mets moment.

Nearly 20 years later, on May 23, 1999, the Mets were being completely shut down—and shut out—by Philadelphia Phillies pitcher Curt Schilling. With Schilling cruising through the Mets' lineup and leading 4–0 going into the bottom of the ninth inning, there was little reason to believe the Mets' bats would suddenly wake up. Heading into the ninth, Schilling had surrendered just 7 singles, hadn't allowed a runner past second base, and had retired nine straight Mets.

Then, just like that, a rally ensued. It all started with a Mike Piazza single and a Robin Ventura blast. Suddenly, it was 4–2. Following a Brian McRae groundout, Matt Franco singled to center, and Luis Lopez was hit by a pitch. That brought up Jermaine Allensworth (remember him?), whose RBI pinch-hit made it 4–3. Roger Cedeño then grounded out, and Schilling was one out away from getting out of a jam and earning the win.

Edgardo Alfonzo came to bat and quickly fell behind in the count, 1–2. Then, Schilling delivered the pitch that would haunt him: he hit Alfonzo to load the bases and bring up the dangerous John Olerud.

"That pitch to Alfonzo ended up burying me," Schilling told reporters after the game. "That's the game . . . I didn't want Olerud up in that spot."

Olerud up in that spot is exactly what Schilling got, however. On the very first pitch to one of the Mets' top hitters, Olerud smacked a game-winning, two-run single to left field to give the Mets a 5–4 victory and Schilling a very unsatisfying complete game.

The Mets did not have another comeback like that until May of 2007, and that one—like the others—seemed highly unlikely. Heading into their mid-May game against the Cubs, Mets manager Willie Randolph decided to rest most of his regulars. It was a day game, one day before the Mets were set to start a three-game series against the Yankees. So Randolph rested David Wright, José Reyes, Carlos Beltrán, and Paul Lo Duca.

"The Cubs aren't even going to show up when they see that lineup," pitcher Tom Glavine joked to reporters before the game.

One Mets starter who was still in the lineup was struggling slugger Carlos Delgado, who was batting just .217 on the young season. When he came to bat in the ninth, Delgado was 0-for-4 with two strikeouts, dropping his batting average to .211. By the time that at-bat ended, Delgado would hit a well-placed bouncing groundball to the right side of the infield and find redemption—but not yet.

Heading into the bottom of the ninth inning, the Mets were trailing the Cubs 6–1. Chicago manager Lou Piniella decided to go with his closer Ryan Dempster (at which point my buddy J. B. and I, having seen enough, went to the Long Island Rail Road platform. We would forever regret the choice we made.).

Dempster started imploding immediately, giving up a leadoff hit to David Newhan, followed by a one-out single to Carlos Gomez. Beltrán then pinch-hit and walked to load the bases. Endy Chavez followed Beltrán with a walk of his own, forcing in a run and making the score 5–2. The bases were still loaded, and the tying runs were now on base. That brought up Ruben Gotay, while Wright and Reyes remained on the bench.

"I'm not going to lie to you," Gotay told reporters after the game, "I thought I was going to be pinch-hit for."

Carlos Delgado celebrates with his teammates after his game-winning hit against the Cubs.

Instead, Gotay remained in the game and singled in a run to make the score 5–3. That was enough for Piniella, who stormed to the mound and took Dempster out of the game—not making eye contact as he took the ball—and brought in left-hander Scott Eyre. In doing so, he forced Randolph to finally go to his bench and call on David Wright—who had never before had a pinch-hit at-bat in his career. That didn't seem to faze him, as he ripped the very first pitch from Eyre into center field for an RBI single to make the score 5–4. Delgado, who put his bat on the ball, subsequently sent a grounder that was just out of the reach of Cubs second baseman Ryan Theriot, scoring two runs and giving the Mets their biggest come-from-behind, walk-off victory since the comeback against Schilling.

Three games, three decades, three walk-offs, three bonus miracle moments. Curtain call.

ACKNOWLEDGMENTS

Without a doubt, the greatest thing about writing this book was getting to speak to so many people who lived these miracle moments firsthand. I was so fortunate to have had so many former players and current broadcasters contribute to this project. Those people included Jay Hook, Jerry Koosman, Jon Matlack, Howard Johnson, Shawn Green, Mark Johnson, Howie Rose, Steve Gelbs, and Ed Randall. I am grateful to each one of them for sharing their memories and—more importantly—their time. Two very good friends—Mark Rosenman and Greg Prime—were instrumental in getting me in touch with some of those men, and for that I am truly thankful.

The very first person I interviewed to for his book was Jay Hook—a true gentleman, who was the winning pitcher in the Mets' first-ever win in 1962. After we finished our conversation about his historic victory against the Pittsburgh Pirates, we just started talking baseball. Jay shared a great story about a conversation he had with sports writer Robert Lipsyte during a rain delay in 1962 about why a curveball curves.

"So I got a pencil and paper and drew a ball and the boundary-level surface and the angular velocities around the ball and the linear velocities going over the ball and explained to him why a curveball curves," said Hook, who—oh yeah—received a master's degree in thermodynamics from Northwestern University. "Of course, who's going to believe a ballplayer about that?" he said with a laugh.

Hook continued to explain to me that after checking with the head of the Physics Department at Columbia University, who agreed with everything he had said, Lipsyte wrote what turned out to be an award-winning article for his paper, the *New York Times*. Two weeks later, after pitching poorly during a start at the Polo Grounds, Hook recounted how he and Lipsyte were in the clubhouse talking when the Mets manager appeared.

"All of a sudden, Casey Stengel walks in, and he looks at me, and he looks at Lipsyte, and said, 'You know, if Hook could only do what he knows.'" Hook said with a hearty laugh. "Since baseball, I have been in business, I have been in academia, I have been active in the church, and have really done so many different things. Almost everything I have done, I have been able to use that quote—'If you could only do what you know.'"

I have tried my best to do what I know in this book—write about the Mets in a fun, interesting way. My favorite part about this book is that it is—in essence—31 short stories, with a constant theme of Mets history connecting all of the stories together. My ultimate goal was to write a book that I would want to read. To that end, I am especially thankful to my editor, Julie Ganz, who not only offered me the opportunity to write this book but also shared my vision on how it should be written.

I could never write a book without the support of my family and friends, and I certainly had plenty of that. Thank you, as always, to my wife and children—Emily, Oliver, and Lily—for their unwavering love and support throughout this project and always; thank you to my mom and dad, who have provided me with everything that makes me me; thank you to Ellen and Steve; Melissa, Jason, Derek, and Kayla; Abigale, David, Cooper, and Quinn—all of whom offer constant unconditional love and support; and to EP and Corinne, who are always there for me. Thank you to Dr. Juhel and everyone at Buckley Country Day School—your kindness and encouragement never ceases to amaze me. Thanks specifically to Theresa, Sam, Brian, Isaac, and John—who served as sounding boards throughout the writing process—and to Liz, who kept me on task with constant encouragement. I also wanted to mention some big-time Mets fans in my life who served as muses without even knowing it—Prof. Fred Rosen, JB, B-Mac, Jon Cheris, Glen Kopp, Jared Smith, Jordan Miller, and Jordan Freundlich. Thank you all. Finally, a special thank you to my friend Ira Podell, a huge Mets fan whose strength and courage is a true inspiration to me.

I really hope, in the end, I was able to do what I know.

SOURCES

Books

Patterson, Ted. *Amazin' Mets: Miracle of 69 (Daily News Legends Series)*. New York: Sports Publishing, 1999.

Pearlman, Jeff. *The Bad Guys Won: A Season of Brawling, Boozing, Bimbo Chasing, and Championship Baseball with Straw, Doc, Mookie, Nails, the Kid, and the Rest of the . . . Put on a New York Uniform—and Maybe the Best*. Reprint edition. New York: Harper Perennial, 2011.

Topel, Brett. *So You Think You're a New York Met's Fan?* New York: Sports Publishing, 2016.

———— *When Shea Was Home: The Story of the 1975 Mets, Yankees, Giants, and Jets*. New York: Sports Publishing, 2015.

Vincent, David. *Home Run's Most Wanted: The Top 10 Book of Monumental Dingers, Prodigious Swingers, and Everything Long-Ball*. Dulles, VA: Potomac Books, 2009.

Newspapers and Websites

Albany Times Union

Amazinavenue.com

Arizona Republic

Associated Press

Baseball-almanac.com

Baseball-reference.com

Binghamton Press and Sun

Centerfieldmaz.com

Cincinnati Enquirer

Daily News (New York)

ESPN.com

The Journal News (Westchester)

Mets.com

Metsmerizedonline.com

MLB.com

New York Times

Newsday

Newspapers.com

SBnation.com

Sky magazine

Sports Collectors Digest

Youtube.com